EFFECTIVE LIBRARY EXHIBITS

HOW TO PREPARE AND PROMOTE GOOD DISPLAYS

SIMPLICITY IN DESIGN —
This type of display is easy and economical to prepare and install.

EFFECTIVE LIBRARY EXHIBITS

HOW TO PREPARE AND PROMOTE GOOD DISPLAYS

By Kate Coplan

Former Chief, Exhibits and Publicity, Enoch Pratt Free Library

Introduction by Gerald W. Johnson

Second Edition

1974 OCEANA PUBLICATIONS, INC. • DOBBS FERRY, NEW YORK

Library of Congress Cataloging in Publication Data

Coplan, Kate.
    Effective library exhibits.

    1. Library exhibits. I. Title.
Z716.3.C774   1974   659.1'9'02   74-4428
ISBN 0-379-00265-5

Manufactured in the United States of America

CONTENTS

CONTENTS (continued)

ILLUSTRATIONS

ILLUSTRATIONS (continued)

If you are in Baltimore, and you wish to know what is going on in the city other than accidents, fires, crimes and equally unpredictable sensations, you have only to take a stroll of one city block on Cathedral Street between Franklin and Mulberry. That block is occupied by the Enoch Pratt Free Library's central building, with twelve show windows, like those of a department store, each window telling a story of something that is occupying the attention of some of the people of Baltimore during the current period.

Is some national fraternity, or trade association, or learned society holding its annual convention in the city? A window will be devoted to the organization, mentioning the meeting and displaying a book — more likely thirty books — on its history and its work. Has a Baltimore author just published a new book? That book will be there, with a bulletin describing it. Is it the anniversary of some historic event? There will be pictures, books, relics of all kinds, relating to the event. Is some other cultural institution — university, college, conservatory, museum, art institute, putting on a special show of some kind? The library will publicize it, and will ransack its own shelves for material bearing on the subject.

In short, here is a visual display of the intellectual life of the city during the three weeks covered. The passer-by with a special interest in one of the subjects has only to step inside the building to find further information and a skillfully assembled collection of printed material relating to it.

The object of this program is first to stimulate and then to satisfy the intellectual curiosity of the Baltimore public, which is, of course, the function of any public library. Evidence of its effectiveness in that regard is the enormous increase in circulation since the system was adopted. But it has had another effect, not so easily measurable, but very great and valuable.

This effect is the integration of the institution with the life of the city ouside its walls. The individual passing along that block may not see in the windows anything of strong and direct interest to him, anything that causes him to pause and study a particular exhibit; but he cannot fail to gain the impression that the library is alive and alert, interested in whatever the citizens of Baltimore are doing, and ready to extend its good offices to help the work along. So when something comes along that does interest him, his steps turn in that direction to see what the library has made of it; and he is usually pleased.

This is one of the strong factors contributing to the vitality of the institution. Time was when the Pratt, like too many other public libraries, was regarded by the public as pretty much a mausoleum of dead ideas, but that was long ago. Today the place is as alive as the post office, and rather more alive than the City Hall. Quiet is enforced in the reading rooms and you can study there very comfortably. But the Pratt is no place for meditation; there is too much going on, and things go on because the people have been made aware of the services that are available in the library.

The idea of assimilating the library into the main current of the city's economic and cultural life was the brain-child of Joseph L. Wheeler, a great librarian; but it has been carefully fostered by Mr. Wheeler's successors in the years since his retirement, and today is going stronger than ever. It is doubtful that there is another big-city library in the country that touches the life of its town more intimately at more points, and this program of salesmanship — for that is what it is — is one of the most important factors in the establishment and maintenance of those contacts.

It is proof of Wheeler's genius that he never did what was expected, but he rarely did anything more surprising than when he entrusted his visual display program to a staff member then a mere slip of a girl. But it was one of his shrewdest appointments. Kate Coplan had no experience in 1927, but she had energy, imagination and, above all, the capacity to learn from her own mistakes, that is to say, the capacity of growth. Through the years, and in the rough but effective school of trial and error, she has matured into a woman who knows as much about this phase of library work as anyone in the United States — some able librarians from other cities have told me that she knows more.

This volume is a distillation of the wisdom that she has been gathering for thirty years. Whether or not it is a contribution to library science I am not competent to decide; but I know beyond peradventure that it is a contribution to library operation, assuming that one aspiration of the library is to be, not a mere adjunct, but a vital, indispensable part of the society to which it belongs.

Nevertheless, it omits one tremendously important step in the creation of a really fine program of visual display, and for the benefit of librarians who consult the volume, and without anybody's permission, I herewith supply that omission. As in the old recipe for rabbit stew, the first direction reads, "first catch your rabbit," so to anyone who envisages a program that shall outshine that of the Enoch Pratt Free Library of Baltimore, I offer this counsel: first catch your Kate Coplan.

— *Gerald W. Johnson*

Baltimore

ACKNOWLEDGMENTS

Since first introduced 15 years ago, this book has fulfilled our fondest hopes. It has gone through 6 printings, proving an important tool in the design and production of more attractive and meaningful library and school exhibits the world over. Moreover, through the good offices of the Committee for a Free Europe, copies have even pierced the Iron Curtain.

Though the volume remains basically sound, it seemed appropriate to revise certain sections, in keeping with developments of recent years. Accordingly, we have replaced a majority of the illustrations contained in the work, inserting contemporary topics among the suggested displays. Also, we have amended the chapter on Library Book Fairs; updated the bibliography; expanded the list of free and inexpensive display materials; added to the sources of supplies and equipment, and appended a new index.

Among the institutions and individuals to whom we are indebted for information and/or assistance in the preparation of this revision are: The Enoch Pratt Free Library in Baltimore; the Randallstown Branch of the Baltimore County Public Library; the Atlantic City Public Library; Miss Howard Hubbard, chief of public relations, Pratt Library, and her staff, particularly William J. Bond and Mr. and Mrs. Charles J. Cipolloni; Miss Sara Siebert, the Pratt's coordinator of young adult services; and Miss Marion Bell, head of that library's reference department; Miss Ruth Tarbox, executive secretary, American Library Association's Young Adult Division; Mrs. Helen K. Wright, of the ALA's Office of Rights and Permissions; Mrs. Alice Rusk, Dr. Edward Goldsmith and Mr. M. Hirsh Goldberg, of the Baltimore City Public Schools; Mr. Raymond O. Trimmer, Maryland Academy of Sciences; staff members of the Maryland Drug Abuse Administration, and Regional Planning Council; Dr. Michael Sherman; Mr. Jack Faw, general manager of the School & Pre-School Supply Center, Inc., Baltimore, and William and Elliott Becker, of the Becker Sign Supply Company in that city. Sincerest appreciation and warmest thanks to all!

— *Kate Coplan*

Baltimore, Maryland
June, 1974

EFFECTIVE LIBRARY EXHIBITS

HOW TO PREPARE AND PROMOTE GOOD DISPLAYS

The modern world has traveled far since the days when people had to depend on lay minstrels, journeying at a snail's pace from village to village, for word-of-mouth news and information.

Today, through a network of libraries, books and information are available for the asking in almost every quarter of the globe. Yet all too few people realize how their everyday lives can be affected and improved by the vast wealth of knowledge which has been accumulated through the centuries and awaits them in books on the shelves of their libraries.

No library, regardless of its size, complexion or financial status, can afford to overlook exhibits as a means of widening its sphere of influence and service. Not only public libraries, but also school and college libraries, industrial libraries, special libraries — all have an opportunity through exhibits to make their readers, present and potential, more aware of their resources and facilities.

Library materials that simply sit on the shelves are just so much dead wood, the money, time and labor expended on their acquisition and processing largely wasted. Through dra-

READING REMINDERS

Although libraries have on their shelves books and information relating to many diversified subjects, only a small percentage of the people in their communities know and draw on the collections. Through eye-catching displays the availability of the various types of printed materials can be emphasized repeatedly, thereby stimulating their use.

Visual presentation has gained continual momentum in recent years. Virtually every field of endeavor — business, industry, agriculture, science, education, even the social services — has stepped up its use of display to interpret its aims and achievements to the public. Certainly libraries, which have so much to offer in the field of education and recreation, cannot lag behind.

matic displays many of these inactive items can be restored to life, thereby fulfilling the authors', publishers' and librarians' intent.

Worthwhile exhibits intelligently presented and enthusiastically promoted, build up an amazing reservoir of good will. They need not cost much, but any investment of funds and staff effort is bound to pay off handsomely in greater usefulness of the materials displayed, and beyond that, in improved public relations and added prestige for the library. Indirectly thereby the library's budget is favorably affected.

I should like to emphasize here that attractive, meaningful exhibits can be produced at relatively low cost. If no separate budget is available for the purpose, there is always the petty cash drawer to fall back on. With ingenuity and resourcefulness, with taste and discrimination, library workers can accomplish creditable displays with minimum outlay.

Many commercial display pieces, their advertising matter judiciously deleted, adapt well to library exhibitions. I remember, years ago, begging an attractive whiskey display that I saw mounted in a tavern window. It featured a high-stepping majorette with baton in hand,

and when the cardboard frame bearing the advertising copy was removed, it made a colorful backdrop decoration for a window display on music.

Baseball figurines from a brewery ad; basketball players from a cigarette ad; oversize paper strawberries from an ice cream manufacturer; tempting food pictures fom a delicatessen — these are some of the items obtained free of charge from Baltimore commercial establishments and adapted for library display purposes.

When we undertook our exhibits program at the Enoch Pratt Free Library back in 1927, we started on the proverbial shoestring. There was no budget, no staff, not even adequate work space.

WIDENING HORIZONS   *While history plays its inevitable part in display programs, the library also has a responsibility to keep readers informed of important current and possible future ideas, discoveries and developments. When atomic energy was "new" the Enoch Pratt Free Library arranged a comprehensive exhibition — in cooperation with the Maryland Academy of Sciences — of which these were the introductory panels.*

2

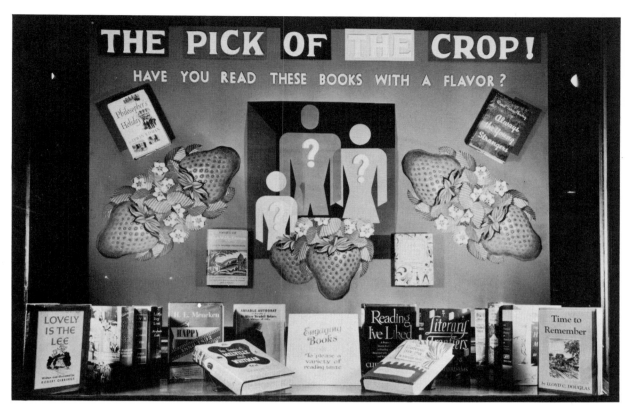

FREE MATERIALS *Many attractive pieces which adapt well to display design may be had free for the asking. In the accompanying illustration are a poster originally issued to advertise the high rate of tuberculosis, and oversize paper strawberries supplied by the Hendler Creamery Company, Baltimore.*

My "office" at the time consisted of a small typewriter table set between two large iron stacks in the old reference room. For fixtures I had the maintenance man build a few small pedestals and tables from odds and ends of lumber lying in the basement. Pieces of discarded wallboard, and cardboard cartons, when covered with gay paper or cheap cloth, served as backdrops and book stands.

Because we had no good areas of our own suitable for displays, Mr. Joseph L. Wheeler, then director, suggested that I borrow vacant store windows in the busy downtown district, to show library materials. After several frustrating attempts, some real estate representatives finally ageed to the temporary loan of a few windows for library displays, provided the FOR RENT signs remained conspicuously placed. (Later, when the rental agents discovered that the exhibits helped lease their properties more quickly, they eagerly sought additional displays.)

A 73-year-old porter on the staff was assigned as my part-time helper. We had no truck or car in those days, and I can picture us still as we walked down the street. On one arm the porter carried a slat basket of books. On the other arm he had a pail and cleaning equipment, for almost invariably the glass of the borrowed windows was so dirty that it was difficult to see through. We always had to beg a bucket of water from the corner drugstore to get the glass washed before each exhibit was installed.

In a position without precedent, one learns by doing. Without proper funds or resources one must improvise, borrow, adapt, stretch whatever is available so it will do double or triple duty. In those early days, to our great surprise and delight — with everything in a given display borrowed except the sign calling attention to the fact that the books were obtainable at the Pratt Library — we won second prize in a national window display contest.

Here in this instance is proof that libraries with even the most limited of funds can embark on a successful exhibits program. Little by little equipment, letter stocks, decorations, will build up until the supply is in satisfactory working order.

One point, however, must be made crystal clear. Library exhibits, to be successful, must be well planned, organized and executed. Amateurish, "home-made" looking displays — whether window displays, bulletin board displays, panel displays, case, table or shelf displays — should be avoided like the plague. Poor lettering, clashing colors, bad art, inexpert arrangement are a discredit, rather than a credit to the library.

Workers without formal art training or natural talent would do well, whenever possible, to enlist the abilities of others. If they can obtain the assistance of advertising specialists, artists or students with a flair for display, the results are likely to be gratifying for both the library and the participants.

Competent students in art classes may contribute posters, show cards and other items for effective exhibits. Vocational classes, and individuals handy with tools, will be glad to turn out small book fixtures and additional pieces of equipment if the "makings" are supplied by the library. In Baltimore we remember with gratitude the early help given by vocational units in the public schools, and by the Maryland Institute.

Few library activities bring the rich rewards that displays do. If they are interesting enough and attractive enough and frequent enough, they can turn many indifferent viewers into active, enthusiastic library users and supporters.

FRUITFUL COOPERATION *Good posters and other display items may be obtained without cost to the library if artists, art students and teachers are invited to cooperate. These posters were among those made as a class project years ago for the Enoch Pratt Free Library, by students of the Maryland Institute.*

4

CHAPTER TWO

DISPLAY IDEAS AND ARRANGEMENT

This is the age of visual education, and libraries must make the most of that fact. Today the most successful agencies everywhere are those which tell the world by every feasible means — especially pictorial presentation — who they are, where they are, what they are doing, why they are doing it and how they are doing it. If the library is to serve as a truly constructive force in the community, then it must make more people aware of how the printed word can help them in their homes, in their jobs, with their educational and recreational problems.

The purpose of library exhibits, of course, is to stimulate interest in books and reading, and to show how the library's services and resources can aid individuals and groups in the community. In the course of a single year a library can place before the public a comprehensive cross-section of its collection, demonstrating how books and other materials tie in with the community's interests.

To the general viewer, a display represents a sampling of what the library has to offer him. All too frequently one observes exhibits distinguished only for lack of novelty, poor art and lettering, or uninteresting design. A display is a good deal like an individual. To be a success in life it must be friendly and appealing, it must have color, balance, personality, and even a sense of humor on occasion. It must please before it can inform. Any exhibit lacking these qualities is likely to fail.

Displays may be devoted to science, art, industry, agriculture, health, literature, business, labor, education, civic and social problems, with emphasis on local achievements in these fields. National and international events, birthdays and deaths of notables, seasonal topics, holidays, commemorative occasions, these are all grist for the display mill. In addition, opportunity is given for the showing of handicraft

DISPLAY IDEAS FOR THE NEW YEAR

Early in January people seem more receptive to suggestions of self-improvement. The "readers" were raised on insulite blocks, to give a three-dimensional quality.

and hobby collections, travelling exhibitions and items from fine private libraries.

Since the displays are to be viewed by persons of all ages, interests and walks of life, the material must be varied in scope and reading level. As in all library activities, an effort should be made to present various points of view, particularly on questions about which there are widely supported, differing shades of public opinion.

Bulletin boards, exhibition cases, free-standing panels, shelves and tables within the library become excellent channels for conveying whatever information the library desires to present. But exterior show windows are far more important, because the chief aim is to carry the reading message to persons not already familiar with the library's facilities and potential usefulness.

UPCOMING HOLIDAYS *Can tie in with a variety of books worthy of display.*

For this purpose well-located window space is essential. A display buried on a side street where there is little pedestrian or motor traffic, is just so much waste of time, effort and energy.

Perhaps the leading grocer on the main street will lend his window for a week or two. As this will represent some sacrifice on his part, the librarian can show appreciation by displaying some tempting cook books, thus promoting not only the books, but also the grocer's wares.

In the spring a hardware merchant might be induced to give up a show window temporarily to an exhibition of garden literature. He will consent with alacrity if a collection of his garden implements can be included in the design. When properly approached almost any shop owner, as a matter of self-interest, will be happy to fall in line with the library's plan.

One almost infallible method for producing a popular exhibit is to include objects lent by some member or members of the immediate community. If 10-year-old Johnny, for example, has built a detailed model of a jet plane, or a teen-age girl has woven a gay rug from old stockings, and you feature these in a handicraft display, success is virtually assured. Not only will the youngsters and their friends make visits to gaze and admire, but so will the doting sisters, brothers, uncles and aunts, not to mention the proud parents.

Also, there is nothing like word-of-mouth advertising. And when Mrs. Smith, oh, so casually, mentions to Mrs. Jones that her Mary is having a rug exhibited by the library, Mrs. Jones will hardly fail to stop by for a look on her way to market.

Ideas for exhibits need not necessarily be

original. Any alert librarian can discover a wealth of suggestions in books, newspapers and magazines, on book jackets, in advertising and publicity journals. A casual walk down the street may yield a number of effective ideas to workers with a seeing eye and a bit of imagination. For instance, a man observed wrestling with the problem of a stalled car at a busy intersection might suggest a display on the care and repair of automobiles. The sight of two corpulent matrons sipping frothy sodas in a drug store might prompt consideration of a display featuring diet and nutrition.

As has been said before, artists and art students, teachers in the community, hobbyists and collectors often may be persuaded to con-tribute ideas, time and material. The more the librarian can get others to do, the less he will have to do himself. Usually ready and willing allies in exhibits undertakings are the public schools.

At the Enoch Pratt Free Library special attention is paid to significant books written by authors presently residing in Baltimore or elsewhere in Maryland. To give recognition and encouragement to local writing talent, the library frequently devotes an entire window exhibit to a single new volume of widespread public interest. Thirty copies of the work are borrowed from the publisher, along with original art, if any, and a photograph of the author, to add a personal touch.

STORE — LIBRARY COOPERATION *A window display in Baltimore's well-known, century-old department store, HUTZLER BROTHERS CO., featuring gardening books from the public library, along with related implements from the store's garden shop. On the back "fence" was posted the following sign: "Whatever your hobby, your job, your research, your travel plans . . . You'll find just the Books to give you 'a lift' at the Enoch Pratt Free Library. Trained librarians are ready to help you."*

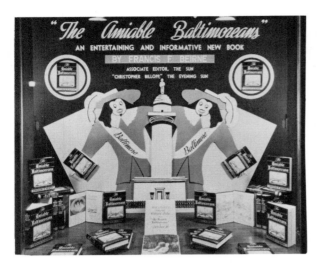

"ASSIST" FOR LOCAL AUTHORS *Through its window displays the Enoch Pratt Free Library gives recognition to significant books by writers presently residing in Baltimore or elsewhere in Maryland.*

Often ready-made exhibits are available for borrowing, with a minimum of effort and labor on the part of the library. Among sources for such displays are schools and colleges, art and science museums, government bureaus, industries, labor unions, transportation and travel agencies. All borrowed materials should be insured against fire, theft and damage, both in transit and while in the library's possession.

In Baltimore it has long been the practice to provide small library exhibits for worthwhile "outside" programs. To name but a few to which the Pratt has sent book displays: child care and training centers; church conferences; United Nations activities; a leadership forum conducted by the Junior Association of Commerce; family affairs institutes and film forums.

EXAMPLE OF A BORROWED DISPLAY

For its second Atomic Energy Institute the Enoch Pratt Free Library borrowed from the American Museum of Atomic Energy at Oak Ridge, Tenn., a fine show, professionally prepared. Shipped to Baltimore in specially-designed crates, the various sections needed only to be set up according to the accompanying instruction chart.

PATHWAY TO PEACE

An exhibition prepared by the Disarmament Staff of the White House, handsomely mounted, and circulated free to cultural institutions around the country.

A display need not be elaborate to be successful. Simple designs are preferable, particularly for beginners.

A small library featuring Bible Week might show a facsimile of a Gutenberg Bible page (probably procurable from Philip C. Duschnes, 699 Madison Avenue, New York, N.Y. 10029, Goodspeed's Book Shop, 18 Beacon Street, Boston, Mass., 02108 or Gutenberg Museum Liebfrauen Platz 5, Rhein Allee, 3, Mainz, Germany). Along with this the exhibition might include Bibles of interest borrowed from persons in the community.

When planning an exhibit, decide upon the central idea, or theme of the display, then build around it. Make a rough preparatory sketch indicating layout and color treatment.

As most librarians are aware, Nicolas Jensen was a Frenchman who served an apprenticeship in the royal mint at Paris, and went to Mainz, Germany, where Gutenberg held forth, to learn the art of printing from movable type at the command of King Charles VII of France. Jensen expected to return to his native land, but following the King's death in 1461, he proceeded to Venice, and is thought by some authorities to have been that city's first printer.

Using Jensen as inspiration, an enterprising librarian could build a convincing display about the France and Italy of his period. No matter how seemingly distant the relationship, "the end justifies the means," and the worker with imagination will invariably find opportunities for linking displays with library services and resources.

AROUND THE WORLD IN 80 BOOKS

An exhibit prepared for a festival of the United Nations Association of Maryland, in cooperation with the Enoch Pratt Free Library's Office of Adult Services. Emphasizing literacy, the charts and signs centered on the theme, "If people can read . . . Books bring the world together."

Whatever the subject emphasized, in the selection of material it is usually wise to include a varied collection of literature, to interest as many types and ages as possible.

Color is a valuable element in any exhibit. When several tones are employed in the design they must harmonize or contrast, but never clash. Workers who claim they have no color sense can study magazine advertisements, as well as bus and trolley cards for pleasing combinations. In summer it is well to emphasize the cooler colors — blues, greens, grays, white, violet. During the winter months the warmer colors — reds, yellows, oranges, etc. — would naturally predominate.

Posters, picture maps, paper jackets on book discards, are always welcome additions to any exhibit, not only for their utilitarian value, but also for their liveliness of color. Photographs, models, action devices, lend added interest.

When choosing literature for a display care must be taken to select books that can be shown to advantage. Good, readable spines, attractive covers and illustrations, clear print for easy reading are all factors to be considered. Often the outer binding of a book may be shabby and dull, but the frontispiece, endpapers or an inside illustration may be gay and inviting. It is up to the librarian to feature the best points of books used in an exhibit.

Whenever possible, book jackets should be used over dummy books — volumes worn out in active service, "freak" or outdated gift books not worth adding. Then the actual volumes may circulate on request. For if a borrower must wait for the publication desired until the display is dismantled, he may lose interest.

"DRESS-UP" DECORATIONS *The appearance of many displays is improved by the use of gay cardboard strips, rectangles, triangles and squares arranged in appealing patterns to offset less colorful backdrop items. The cutter demonstrated here can take a full 28 x 44 inches sheet of cardboard. Circles up to 24 inches in diameter may be produced with a special attachment on the *Cutawl machine.*

(*See Preparation and Techniques).

PAINTING BULLETIN BOARDS AND DISPLAY BACKDROPS

For a smooth finish mix water paint well, and with a four-inch brush stroke the paint evenly up and down across the board. This will prevent streakiness.

Every exhibit should have a backdrop that is eye-catching, to stop people in their tracks. The aim is to make each library exhibit so irresistible that passers-by, who read as they run, will come back for a second and longer look. At the Enoch Pratt Free Library portable insulite (wallboard) panels, reinforced with 2 by 4 wooden frames to prevent warping, are used for the purpose. Self-supporting on small wood feet, they are covered with quick-drying water paints and adorned with attractive books and related cardboard decorations.

Three-dimensional cutout letters, painted to set off the rest of the design, are carefully spaced out and measured for the caption or message.

As to arrangement, avoid clutter. It is well to remember that no matter how great the variety of pieces involved, the display must not appear crowded or jumbled. Each item should be placed so that it may be plainly seen. No one piece should be permitted to obscure another. The more significant books should be placed most strategically, but the entire exhibit must present a certain symmetry and balance.

There should always be sufficient "white space," to use the printer's term. For if an exhibit appears crowded or disjointed, it will hardly attract attention, much less create interest or stimulate the desire to read which, after all, is the primary purpose of the display.

After a display has been completed it should be examined carefully for flaws. Perhaps a book is upside down, a label out of line, or an object off balance. Minor adjustments are almost always necessary.

11

INSULITE DISPLAY PANELS *Such items are easy to construct. Insulite, a wood-pulp wall board ½ inch thick, can be purchased in almost any lumber yard, in 4 x 8 foot sheets. It takes paint and pins readily, but must be protected from knocks and bumps, as it chips and scars easily. A 2 x 4 frame on the back of the panel prevents warping. After the panel has been painted and decorated, free-standing feet may be bolted on, for greater stability.*

SELECTING CAPTION LETTERS

The amount of display space and the material to be featured determine the size and style of the caption letters. A large space naturally calls for larger letters, and bulky display pieces used in an exhibit also would demand big letters. On the other hand, fragile china or handmade jewelry would call for a caption composed of "refined," graceful letters. Shelves or boxes divided into compartments do nicely for storing letter alphabets.

PAINTING LETTERS

At the Enoch Pratt Free Library quick-drying water paints in colors that harmonize or contrast with other display features are used extensively for exhibits captions. If its edges are coated first, each letter can then be held on the palm of the hand and the face painted. Lay on a smooth, hard surface to dry.

SPACING OF LETTERS

Three-dimensional letters used in display captions must be evenly aligned and spaced out as meticulously as a page of hand-set type. A long, thin strip of wood temporarily tacked onto the working area below the letters, will keep the bottoms of the letters on an even keel. Spaces between letters, as well as spaces between words, should be equalized. (Letters placed on contrasting cardboard strips generally show up to advantage). Until experience has developed a "straight eye," a measuring guide should be used.

13

CHAPTER THREE

PREPARATION AND TECHNIQUES

Keeping in mind the keen competition for the public's attention these days, every library display must be attractive and eye-catching if it is to fulfill its function. This chapter will deal with some of the mechanics for achieving that aim. Materials mentioned may be checked in the appendix, under Sources of Supplies.

For instance, if two corners of a book jacket or leaflet are affixed firmly to a bulletin board with thumb tacks, while the remaining two flap loosely in the breeze every time the door opens, the display loses much of its appeal.

And speaking of thumb tacks — avoid using different colored heads on a single display

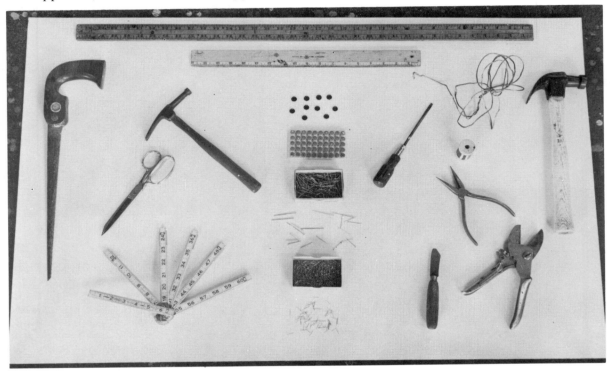

TOOLS OF THE TRADE *Pictured here are a few simple working tools useful in the preparation of exhibits. Measurements should be accurate, neatness is indispensable.*

One of the first requirements of good display is neatness. Unless an exhibit is neat, it cannot look attractive, and if it is not attractive, it will not get attention. Certainly it goes without saying that unless an exhibit draws attention, it will hardly stimulate reading interest, with the result that most of the time and money spent in its preparation are virtually wasted.

piece! When a small white announcement is attached to a bulletin board with a red, a green, and two steel thumb tacks — as I have seen done — the result is nothing more than a hodgepodge. Don't use the more expensive but less attractive steel or brass tacks to make display pieces become joined to a surface, if you can obtain others which fit more harmoniously into the design. When thumb tacks are to show, get colors to match the display materials, or paint white ones the proper shade, so they will not be a disturbing factor.

If possible fasten things with pins (available in sizes ranging from ½ inch to 2 or more inches, depending on the requirements of the job at hand), and then touch up the tiny pinheads with matching paints, so that they will blend unobtrusively into the items featured.

BOOK DISPLAY EQUIPMENT

Examples of items used by the Enoch Pratt Free Library. Some are more than 25 years old.

AFTER DECORATION

Dummy books in paper jackets conceal most of the wooden pedestals and tables in Pratt Library displays.

15

Wooden boxes, pedestals, blocks — painted or varnished to suit the surroundings — and small wrought iron or wooden troughs, will serve admirably as book display fixtures. Varisized cartons and other containers, obtained from neighborhood stores likely to discard them, can be covered with odds and ends of wallpaper, gay wrapping paper, metal foil or low-priced cloth to make presentable book stands.

Ordinary metal book supports, placed at a 45 degree angle or bent to any other height desired, can also be pressed into service as "fixtures." But when adjoining books are placed on such supports, they should be at similar levels, for if one is projected higher than the other, the area will offer a ragged appearance.

In addition, book supports may be used straight to prop up books that have a tendency to fall over. Insert these in the back of the volumes, with the tongue-like base pointing toward the rear of the display, in line with the idea that "props" — devices by which material is shown to its best advantage — must always be as inconspicuous as possible.

Valuable manuscripts, old letters and other exhibits susceptible to the sun's rays, may be wrapped in amber cellophane to prevent fading. For a firm base and minimum buckling, place a piece of cardboard cut to size under each piece before wrapping.

Narrow white cotton tape, inexpensive when obtained in 1000-yard spools, is useful for tying books open. Cut two strips a little longer than twice the height of the book to be opened and place them on the outer margins, tying the ends at the back. Snip off the long ends, so they will not protrude. Make sure the tape strips are about ¼ inch from the edge, top

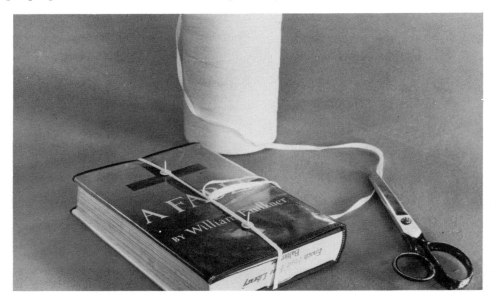

ATTACHING BOOKS WITH TAPE *Attaching a book to a bulletin board or display backdrop is a simple procedure. Insert narrow cotton tape between the paper jacket and front cover, knotting ends at center back. Then below and above the knot, as indicated, insert two upholstery tacks, pushing through the tape with points facing out. Snip off tape ends with scissors and press the book into the desired position, the points penetrating the backdrop. Two long pins placed beneath the book will keep it from sagging to right or left.*

and bottom. (Rubber bands, sometimes employed by librarians for this purpose, detract from the appearance of the book and have a tendency to break when temperatures mount, looking like so many worms on the floor of the exhibit.)

The narrow white tape is also useful for attaching books to display backdrops. In each case cut a length of tape somewhat longer than twice the height of the book. Slip it between the jacket and the front cover of the dummy book, pull taut and knot the tape ends at the center back of the book. Snip off excess ends. Above and below the knot, about six inches apart, insert two upholstery tacks, the points pushed through the tape and facing away from the book. Then press the volume onto the backdrop, in the position desired. Two steel pins

placed directly below the bottom book corners will prevent sagging and will help support the piece.

When working with specially fine books, or books with full-page illustrations, use ½ inch clear, non-adhesive plastic or acetate strips to hold the volumes open. These can be cut from material available in sheets of 40 x 60 inches, or by the yard. Place at page edges, instead of the white tape, and fasten ends at the back of each book with small metal OK clips available in stationery stores.

Occasionally a sheet of tissue paper protects the frontispiece of a book to be displayed, obscuring the illustration. After the book has been tied open, roll the tissue gently but tightly, and fasten it carefully to the center of the book with regular paper clips. The thinner

REINFORCING WITH CARDBOARD *To prevent curling, reinforce pamphlets, magazines, pictures, leaflets and newspaper clippings with cardboard. Two pieces, only very slightly smaller than page size, are inserted in each pamphlet or magazine. Clear, non-adhesive acetate strips cut into ½ inch widths are placed on the outer page edges, so as not to cover printing, and fastened with metal OK clips, holding the concealed cardboard in place. Except for single page items, when there is no alternative, OK clips should be placed where they will not show.*

part of the clip is inserted into the cigarette-type roll, top and bottom. Do not close the book after this treatment, as the tissue will crease. When the display is dismantled, remove the paper clips and flatten the tissue before removing the tapes and closing the book.

Flimsy pamphlets, pictures and newspaper clippings should be reinforced with cardboard before being placed in an exhibition, to prevent curling. To reinforce a pamphlet cut two pieces of old cardboard slightly smaller than page size. Place the colored side of the cardboard away from public view, thus insuring that it will not be conspicuous if the cardboard should slip a bit later. Cut two ½ inch wide clear plastic strips the desired length, and fasten with OK clips on the inside of the pamphlet if the cover is to be shown. When a pamphlet is to be opened, the OK clips should be at the back, in line with the need to conceal "props."

To reinforce an inexpensive photograph or flat paper, cut cardboard the exact size of the item. Fasten the four corners with small OK clips, the sharp prongs piercing the cardboard. Valuable materials may be tied with strips of the clear plastic tape at the outer edges (similar to those used on open books) with OK clips fastening the strips at the back.

If it is necessary for a piece thus handled to stand upright, attach to the reinforcement, center back, a strip of cardboard about 3 inches wide, flush with the bottom and about 2½ inches down from the top edge. Paste only the upper fourth of the strip, leaving the lower section as an easel.

To affix a photograph or picture to a bulletin

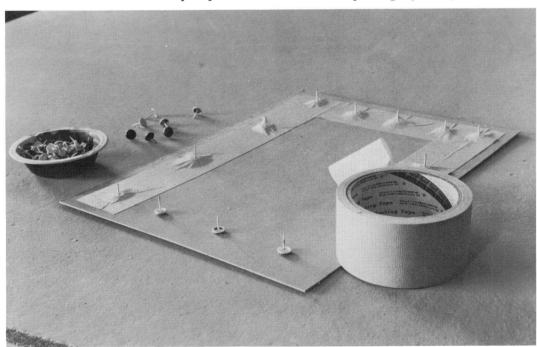

PROTECTING PICTURES *Valuable photographs, drawings and other pictorial items may be affixed to bulletin boards without puncturing holes in the corners. In each case, turn the display piece face down on a work table. Depending upon its weight, place thumb tacks or upholstery tacks at intervals near the edge all around, prongs pointing up, then cover the heads with strips of masking tape, as shown in the accompanying photograph. When the masking tape "border" is complete, the protruding points are pressed into position on the bulletin board.*

18

board without visible means and without puncturing holes in the corners, turn the display piece face down on a work table. Lay as many thumb tacks or upholstery tacks as seem necessary about 3 inches apart and about ½ inch from the edge all around, prongs pointing up. Then make a border with masking tape, covering the heads of the tacks and allowing only the sharp prongs to protrude. The picture can then be pressed into position on the bulletin board.

Persons without formal art training or talent can nevertheless turn out attractive display decorations by incorporating into the design enlargements of illustrations encountered in book jackets, books, magazines, pamphlets, posters or leaflets. Credit, of course, should always be given.

To enlarge a drawing by the squaring method, choose the illustration which you wish to present as the eye-catching device for your exhibit. Draw a perfect square around the illustration. Then with pencil and ruler divide this square into ½ inch squares.

Determine the size of the enlargement desired. If your backdrop illustration is to be four times the original size, then another square is drawn, four times the size of the first one. This time, with your pencil and ruler draw your lines at 2 inch intervals until the whole area is taken care of. Next, in the proportion of the original illustration, draw in your picture, block by block, as seen in the ½ inch squares. Do not worry about the overall pattern, but duplicate the lines in each square exactly, and the larger drawing will come out the same as the original. Cutouts, as well as drawings, can be done in this way.

On occasion, also, enlarged photostatic reproductions of sharp half-tones and black-and-white drawings make good display decorations when mounted on wallboard.

ENLARGING BY THE SQUARING METHOD

Small drawings found in books, magazines and pamphlets can be "blown up" effectively for posters and display decorations. By dividing the original into small squares and duplicating the individual block lines in proportionately bigger squares, an exact enlargement is achieved. Credit should always be given.

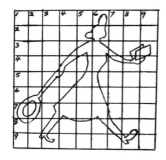

A workbox containing hammer, folding rule, pliers, scissors, dust cloths, thumb and upholstery tacks, assorted pins and nails, OK and paper clips, clear and cotton tape strips, touch-up paints, glue, art gum and other display paraphernalia is required equipment. Those libraries which can afford a Cutawl machine for cutting caption letters and display decorations, will find it a tremendous advantage over scissors, razor blades, knives and other elementary cutting tools. Taking material up to an inch in thickness, the Cutawl will produce at one time several sets of letters in 14-ply (⅛ inch) cardboard, as well as attractive designs related to books and reading, thereby greatly enhancing the exhibits.

Some cautions and reminders:

Exhibits should be designed and presented in such a way that they are self-explanatory

When fitting paper jackets on "dummy" books, be sure you have a snug fit — check for height, depth and width of spine, so that the volumes will appear genuine

To gain a three-dimensional effect with cardboard decorations, place pieces of insulite behind them and attach to the bulletin board or exhibits backdrop with long pins

WORK TRUCK

Equipment required for display preparation and installation is handy to use if assembled compactly in an accessible spot. A book truck, if available, serves admirably for this purpose, as it can be moved at will.

Bend pin points over with pliers where they protrude dangerously. Do not let insulite edges show

Remove and file book cards of actual books used in displays, with a note as to when the displays are to be dismantled, in order to answer inquiries and take reserves from readers

Keep a record of all exhibits by lender, subject, date

Have a "possibilities" file of material offered for loan, for future reference

Save all signs, posters, letters, decorations, cardboard circles, triangles, etc., for later showings in somewhat different form

Take good care of equipment, storing it properly when not in use

CUTAWL MACHINE

Display decorations in almost every conceivable pattern can be made with the versatile Cutawl machine. Patterns may be drawn on brown wrapping paper, and laid over the material to be cut. A few pins driven in will hold both in place during the cutting process. The chisel-like "knife" is guided along the drawn lines. The Cutawl will take material up to an inch in thickness, and special blades for cutting wood and metal are available. If the design is to include several colors, the pieces can be put together like a jigsaw puzzle, with gummed paper on the back. To prevent warping, cover the finished cutout with clean paper, weight down, and press overnight.

CHAPTER FOUR

POSTERS, SIGNS AND SHOWCARDS

Just as a chain is no stronger than its weakest link, so an exhibit is no better than its posters, signs and showcards. Regardless of how many fine features a display may boast, inferior posters and lettering will lower the level of the effort, spoiling the overall effect and leaving viewers with a bad impression.

placed in such a way that comprehension is quick and clear. Color masses must be pleasing, well-balanced.

Libraries lacking competent art staff or volunteer artists, may want to invest in an enlarging projector — such as that put out by Charles Beseler Company — for "blowing up" suitable

IN PRAISE OF POSTERS

Posters are the hardy perennials of library displays. If well executed they serve to win attention and to stimulate interest in books and reading. Color, size, design and lettering are the principal elements to consider. In addition to paints, charcoal, crayons and the other familiar media, novel effects may be achieved by using construction paper scissor-cutouts for illustrations (attached with rubber cement) and adding ink-line finishing touches. The poster in foreground is an example of the latter treatment.

Posters, signs and showcards used in an exhibit should supplement and tie in with the principal caption. Together they tell the library's story, and carry the message.

After determining the size and color preference of each piece as part of the whole, consider the design, or layout. Design is an orderly plan of arrangement. It guides the eye from one element to another, with stopping places for emphasis, to a logical climax. The words and illustrations should be grouped and

illustrations available in their collections. (Some of these gadgets also reduce the size of pictures when such treatment is desired.)

Novices in poster art may also find helpful the instructions on enlarging drawings by the squaring method, given in the chapter, PREPARATION AND TECHNIQUES.

All hand-lettering must be distinct, direct and easy to read, with minimum wordage necessary to accomplish its purpose. The style should conform as far as possible to the exhibits

**INFORMATION
ATTRACTIVELY PRESENTED**

Descriptive showcards, signs and labels call for special skills and talents. The competent showcard writer is usually a versatile artist who varies his pen and brush lettering styles to suit the exhibits being offered. Under no circumstances should crude, "home-made" signs and explanatory notes be used in a library display. They will counteract the good impression created by the exhibit proper.

When professionally-done, hand-lettered labels are not obtainable, typed ones may be used. Space with care, and see that the typewriter ribbon is in good condition, for maximum legibility.

theme. For example, a Shakespearean display would call for a variation of Old English lettering, while a show devoted to abstract art would demand modern lettering. Copy should be "short and snappy" — brief enough to be read quickly, and interesting enough to win and hold attention.

Librarians whose budgets can stand the strain would be wise to have experts do their lettering work, if they have no way of getting free professional assistance. Often showcard writers in department stores or free lance display workers will take on such added chores, to make extra money in their spare time. In

this way the library gets the benefit of reduced rates. Once you have conveyed your ideas to an experienced sign and poster man, given him the copy and indicated sizes, let him use his own initiative. The chances are he will improve considerably on your suggestions.

For those who wish to investigate other possibilities there are available lettering guides, such as the Wrico lettering stencils, and the expensive card-writing equipment — Showcard Machine, Lino-O-Scribe and Print-A-Sign.

On occasion three-dimensional cutout letters may be employed successfully for poster messages. These letters can be acquired for pennies.

Alphabets are obtainable in various sizes, styles and materials. For libraries forced to practice rigid economy it is generally good policy to limit purchase to one style. Variety may be achieved by combining two or three sizes of the same type.

Cheapest and perhaps most useful for the library display purposes are the durable die-cut letters. These range from the very thin Mutual Aids, adhesive and non-adhesive, to the thicker Hallcraft, Redicut and others. They may be had in special fonts or sets, with the proper assortment of vowels and consonants, for adequate service. Some choice of color is available, and in a few cases purchasers may order script letters as well as Roman; lowercase letters, as well as capitals.

(Photo courtesy of The Baltimre Sunpapers)

GIFT POSTERS   *For special campaigns outside agencies and individuals can sometimes be persuaded to underwrite poster projects. Years ago hundreds of copies of this poster were donated by The Joseph Katz Company, Advertising, for the Enoch Pratt Free Library's first branch bond issue in Baltimore.*

23

CHAPTER FIVE

TIPS TO TEACHERS

School teachers and teacher-librarians have a wonderful opportunity, as well as a great responsibility. It lies within their province not only to teach children how to read, but also how to think.

Young minds are curious, receptive minds. It is up to teachers and librarians to feed them a nutritious mental diet. Boys and girls who learn to read with discrimination early in life, generally grow into good citizens, mature in thought and action.

Visual displays are now ranked among the foremost educational aids. Classroom, as well as library exhibits, can be arranged in such a way as to tell an interesting story. History and geography can be made dramatic and colorful for the student who despises both. Zoology can be made appealing to the girl who squirms at the mere mention of a worm. Through effective exhibits even the "driest" subjects can become understandable and arresting.

Who knows but that it may be a book in

POSTER TRANSFORMED

The family group in this "home" setting originally appeared on a poster issued by a manufacturer of light bulbs. Strips of donated wallpaper were used for the background, and the "curtains" were made from shelf paper bought in the five-and-dime store.

GOOD BOOKS

FROM THE CHILDREN'S ROOM ON MULBERRY ST.

TO READ ALOUD

24

one of your displays that will light the spark of scientific discovery in a boy, and inspire him to become a benefactor of mankind? Pasteur, Westinghouse and many other notables were spurred to their achievements by reading.

A sure-fire method of producing a popular school exhibit is to show objects loaned by pupils or their parents. Encourage such co-operation, drawing on selective handicraft and hobby collections. Get your art classes interested, and if there are shop courses in your school some boys handy with tools will gladly assist with the project.

Participation intensifies interest. If it seems feasible, appoint an exhibition committee. The students can help plan and prepare the displays, and by pooling ideas and resources, you may get some valuable support. Change the personnel of your committee periodically, in order to give as many youngsters as possible an opportunity to share actively in the program. More and more they will come to feel a personal responsibility for the exhibits, and their interest and enthusiasm will grow proportionately.

Naturally the children will discuss the displays in their homes, and among their friends. The popularity of the exhibits will mount accordingly. In addition, if you can accommodate visitors, inform neighborhood individuals and groups that would not ordinarily hear about the show.

In the event of a special Shakespearean display, for example, notify local literary clubs. Post notices about your exhibit on the bulletin boards of churches in your area, on store counters, at fairs, and wherever else numbers of people are likely to see them.

By all means get reports of your exhibit into the daily and weekly newspapers. There is a good deal of truth in the old saying, "Nothing succeeds like success." Accounts of your exhibits in the newspapers will impress readers with the importance of what you are doing.

CASE DISPLAY

Locomotive models augment the showing of railroad books for children.

Children's librarians report that boys and girls prefer exhibits projecting things and topics that are familar. They also welcome dramatic, imaginative arrangements, and appreciate well-planned, attractively-presented though simple, exhibits.

Central characters denoting action are always juvenile favorites. Color is important. At the Enoch Pratt Free Library two extremes in intensity seem to register well — pale pastels combined with deep, vibrant tones. Youngsters appear to favor neat, crisp, uncluttered displays and posters, with captions short and to the point.

A successful display recently reported by the Edmondson Avenue Branch featured "MEN OF IRON." This dramatized two 10″ figurines, knights in battle. One, vanquished, was lying prone, his shield and sword beside him. The victor, bending over the fallen man, stood with sword raised, ready to give the final thrust. Books on chivalry were placed at strategic points. The knights wore armor fashioned from aluminum foil, and the banner and backdrop were deep purple. Cutout silver letters comprised the caption.

"CIRCUS DAYS" was the title of an exhibit depicting miniature clowns equipped with the oversize wooden shoes characteristic of real clowns. The head of one Big Top jester was seen bursting through a drum.

A spooky "GHOSTS AND GOBLINS" display contained store-bought Hallowe'en masks — a devil and a ghost with streamer confetti — along with appropriate books. According to Mrs. Freda Freyer, children's librarian, "It was the shivery-looking caption-letters cut from cardboard by the Exhibits staff, that did the trick. We use them from year to year."

Youngsters enjoy sly humor behind ideas and captions. For her display, "IT'S NEARLY SPRING," Mrs. Freyer used letters spelling out the theme above a book bin decorated with a picture from an old *Jack and Jill* Magazine. The illustration showed an elf protecting himself from the rain by holding a toadstool umbrella. When, later, the vernal equinox occurred, Mrs. Freyer superimposed a large paper X on the heading's middle word, thus deleting the "nearly." Commented some of the youthful patrons, "Say, that's plenty neat."

GINGERBREAD HOUSE

At the Enoch Pratt Free Library's Edmondson Avenue Branch this "Hansel and Gretel" cake-and-candy structure added considerable interest to a display of fairy and folk tales.

(Photo by Walter McCardell, The Sunpapers, Baltimore).

From time to time children enjoy "quiet" arrangements — displays devoid of apparent action stimulus, but pleasant to look at. A cake-and-candy "gingerbread" house reminiscent of Hansel and Gretel, as a foil for fairy and folk tales, is worth all the time and effort expended. Beatrix Potter figurines — Peter Rabbit and the rest — are always well received.

Those teachers who cannot create authentic-looking three-dimensional replicas of book characters, gingerbread houses and similar items for exhibits, or who cannot obtain them from other sources, may resort to using paper silhouettes, which are easy to make.

In connection with a display of books about Columbus and other explorers, Mrs. Freyer cut white paper silhouettes of the Nina, the Pinta and Santa Maria. She placed these in progression of size — to create the illusion of sailing into the distance — on deep blue paper with pristine white letters spelling out the caption, "SAIL ON."

Seasonal displays usually have a host of admirers. At the Edmondson library "I LIKE WINTER" combined a vivid blue background with lots of white: snow, snowballs, snow men, snow crystals cut from dull white paper. Icicles dripped from the caption letters.

Frequently pictorial art in giveaway posters can be cut and mounted attractively for bulletin boards and display backdrops. United Nations posters are among those which adapt particularly well to this treatment.

Catchy book titles often make good display captions. For example, the exhibit "MEN OF IRON" was taken from Howard Pyle's book of the same title, and "I LIKE WINTER" was suggested by Lois Lenski's well-known volume.

Exhibiting collection or hobby items always brings offers of additional material. Children enjoy collections of dolls, stamps, sea shells, puppets, almost anything. Another child's work is always meaningful to youngsters. Related

WALLPAPER COSTUME

Simple display designs appeal to children. The girl's wallpaper dress was easy to cut and pin, and paper doilies provided the "lace" trimming."

POSTER CUTOUTS

Many attractive display designs can be contrived with a little resourcefulness. This backdrop center piece was cut from a United Nations poster duplicating the one illustrated.

articles supplementing the books invariably serve as "bait" to draw attention.

For an exhibit in Baltimore involving David Livingstone, the Scottish explorer, an African shield, spears, war hatchet, bow, arrows and quiver were borrowed. A display centering on "ALICE IN WONDERLAND" included puppets representing various characters in the story. Stuffed and mounted birds, nests and eggs were obtained for an exhibit devoted to bird habits and habitats.

Do not hesitate to request the loan of such material. Local individuals and groups are unfailingly cooperative, particularly where the education of children is concerned. Of course, all borrowed properties must be handled with scrupulous care, and returned safely to the owners.

Following are some additional display topics which have appealed to Baltimore boys and girls: astronomy; the story of transportation; sports; photography; wild flowers; historic trails across the United States; camping; paper making; fossils; rockets; bees; foreign trade; Indian artifacts; bird houses; current events; the story of spices; poisonous plants; patents; sea stories; steel; bottle making; marionettes; minerals; prehistoric animals; care of pets; the National Parks; safety; Eskimos; weather.

Mrs. Freyer sums it all up this way: "The philosophy of trying to achieve effective exhibits with the two-fold purpose of providing entertainment and promoting good books is to have colorful, simple displays, with an occasional elaborate one sandwiched in when a busy schedule permits.

"Think about what you want to 'sell'; decide when is the right time to present the display. Be aware, ahead of time, of neighborhood interests and activities, holidays, seasons, events that you may care to observe, always tying in with appropriate reading. Then present the ideas in ways that you know are appealing to young minds."

FOR TEACHERS AND PARENTS
The Enoch Pratt Free Library works closely with Baltimore's public schools, displaying publications tying in with their special reading programs. For their part, the public schools list important library exhibits and activities in their calendar of events, and cooperate in many other ways.

CHAPTER SIX

LIBRARY BOOK FAIRS:
Introduction to "A World of Books"

Note: This chapter is largely based on "Blueprint for a Book Show," written for the American Library Association's Young Adult Services Division by Miss Sara Siebert, enterprising coordinator of Young Adult Services at the Enoch Pratt Free Library in Baltimore. Although originally presented some years ago, the ideas and suggestions featured are as pertinent and practical today as when they were first initiated. Of course, where preferred, other titles, music and decor may be substituted for those mentioned. The show at the Pratt was redesigned many times, to keep it reasonably current. Grateful thanks are herewith tendered to both Miss Siebert and ALA's Miss Ruth Tarbox for their gracious permission to incorporate the material.

Before side show barkers and patent medicine men become just curious relics of America's social past, one should give these fellows their due. Professionally speaking, they were smart boys, forerunners of the Madison Avenue crowd. With a funny gag, a startling statement, and a running patter that fascinated an audience this side of hypnotism, they caught the ears, eyes, and often the silver which jingled in the pockets of even disinterested on-lookers.

Substitute sincerity and honest know-how for slickness, library materials for bearded ladies or patent cure-alls, and the questioning minds of teen-agers for the gullibility of a side show audience — and librarians have a quick, colorful, lively means of introducing young adults to the infinite resources of the library.

For many years the Enoch Pratt Free Library of Baltimore used this Book Fair idea and adaptations of it in programs both in the library and within the community. Probably the most ambitious and longest running activity involving the technique were the fairs arranged annually for 10th, 11th or 12th grade classes in the public high schools of the city. The first of these was colorfully described by Miss Grace P. Slocum, now assistant director of the Pratt Library, but then one of the

Pratt's young adult librarians who helped plan, design and run the early fairs. Although the events were subsequently updated numerous times, Miss Slocum's early description as published in the *Library Journal* provides a good bird's-eye view of the overall activity. She wrote:

"In the Patterson Park area of East Baltimore, where children read some, young people read little and adults read even less, the neighborhood branch librarian approached the head of the English department of the nearby high school to consider how the seniors could be made aware of what the public library could offer them after they left school. Something more was needed than book talks in the classroom in this community, where many students had never set foot in the library. Tentative plans were therefore made for the English classes to visit the branch during school hours.

"Obviously, a routine program on library use would bore these seniors to death. A light touch was needed. A carnival type show seemed to be the answer.

"The library carpenter built eight collapsible booths which could easily be disassembled and stored for future use. The booths measured 60 inches across and 74½ inches high in front, the roof sloping up to a height of 87 inches in the rear. Of the 49 inches in depth, 25 were used for a counter under which was built a shelf for extra books, and the remaining 24 inches were left for standing room (for a 'Y' librarian). Each booth was painted a different color and covered with green and red striped awning top.

"The downstairs meeting room of the branch where the fair was to be held had recently been painted, but the exposed pipes and radiators suspended midway up the walls presented problems. By cutting strips of crepe paper two inches wide, in three different colors, an attractive plaid design covered the pipes, making an effective border around the top of the room.

"Balloons were hung from the ancient, unsightly light fixtures. Thus lighted up, the balloons

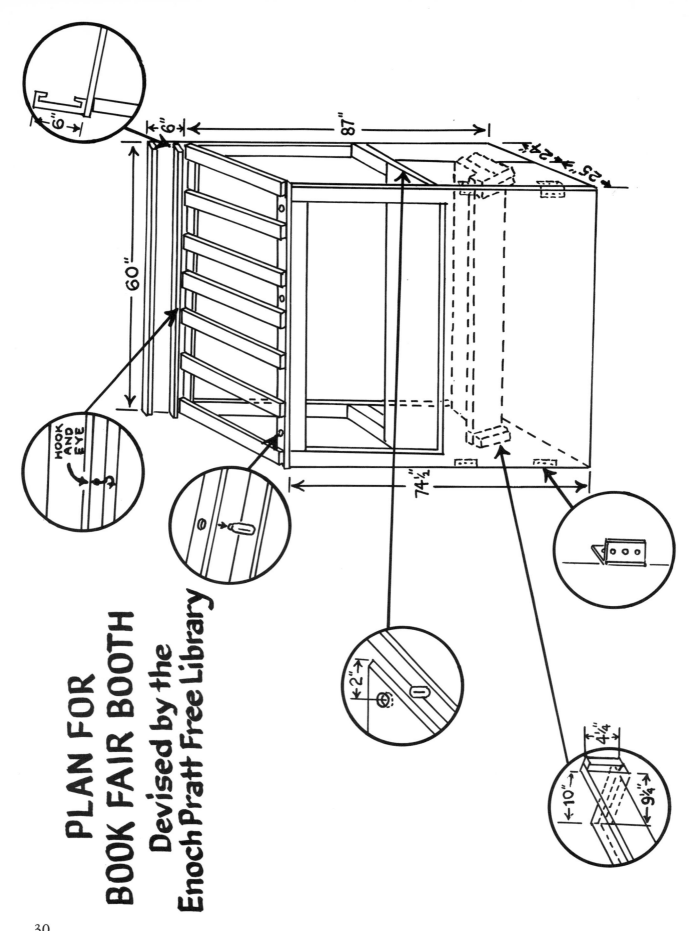

PLAN FOR
BOOK FAIR BOOTH
Devised by the
Enoch Pratt Free Library

HOOK AND EYE

87"

25" x 24½"

6"

6"

60"

74½"

2"

10"

4¼"

9¼"

30

seemed to be incandescent. Three booths were lined up on either side of the room, with the remaining two back to back in the center. The hobby table was placed in the alcove at the rear of the auditorium; the stage at the front was used for the music and dance exhibits.

"On the Monday morning when the first class of seniors arrived at 9 o'clock, they were surprised to be asked to go downstairs, and still more surprised when they began to hear the opening music from 'An American in Paris.' Balloons, serpentine

and crepe paper streamers, along with booths and music, created a carnival atmosphere. Leaflets announcing the carnival of books and listing the library's services were handed out at the door. On the back of the handbills was a notice that a prize would be given away each day — (in those pre-inflation days, any book in the fair costing $5.00 or less) — to the person presenting the best reason for wanting the book.

"The Patterson Park assistant, as Master of Ceremonies, stood on the stage and pointed out

DECORATED BOOK FAIR BOOTH

The gay striped awning top and colorful decorations help create a carnival-like atmosphere, setting the stage for the book display.

each booth, where the 'Y' librarian in charge briefly explained his part of the show. After reminding the seniors to try for the prize, and saying that any of the books . . . could be borrowed on either a student's name or his card, the M.C.

declared the carnival officially opened.

"The backdrop of the first booth, *Choosing a Career,* featured the cutout of a mother kangaroo whose young son had been riding free too long. At the end of her patience, she was demanding,

'Don't you think it's time you got yourself a job?' Here were displayed up-to-date pamphlets and books on vocations and opportunities in the armed forces.

"In the booth, *Personality Merry-Go-Round,* a revolving carousel carried gold horses and books on etiquette and psychology, the best in dating and family living.

"Red brick paper and English ivy decorated the college booth where catalogs from seventy-five colleges and universities could be checked out, with information on how to select a school, or why go to college. Guides for the 'prom-trotter' and a collection of new college stories were included with the more serious material."

Design for Living introduced the booth on home decoration and planning efficiency; *Laugh Like Anything* was the humor caption; *Anyone Can Paint* presented fine arts publications; *Ride Your Hobby* offered literature ranging from stamp collecting to taxidermy.

"The heads of the English departments in all the city's high schools," Miss Slocum explained, "were invited to the carnival. They came, some expecting to find a well-meant but amateurish show, but remained charmed by the almost professional tone. But more than that, they were pleased — as the library staff was pleased — to find young people in a community generally thought to be made up of non-readers, handling books with interest and finding in them ideas related not only to their present daily interests, but also to their future lives."

"SALES PITCH" TO YOUNG ADULTS *The Pratt Library's book fair became a "Baltimore institution" in the city's high schools, with hundreds of seniors attending annually.*

In true carnival fashion, barkers were assigned to ballahoo the books of the various sections. Each chose six or seven volumes ahead of time, and when his turn came he had these readily at hand so that he might point out briefly and succinctly the best features of each. As a particular book was discussed, it was held high for all the visitors to see.

The career booth was stocked with "how-to" handbooks, general vocational materials, specific advice on diversified careers, as well as creative and popular literature. The barker's lively patter drew and held the attention of listeners. It went this way:

"Unless you can break yourself of the bad habit of eating, most of you will go to work within the next five years. Do you know how to write or apply in person for a job? What facts about yourself should you have in hand for your first interview? 'How to Get and Hold the Job You Want,' by Ruth Larison (he held the book high) answers these questions in a logical, unique way by taking applicants through ten steps to a job — from a listing of what one has to offer an employer, to the interview follow-up."

Then, holding up another work — "This heavy, thick tome is the 'Occupational Outlook Handbook,' a United States government publication that covers over 500 occupations and industries. In the index you can find not only the usual vocations — lawyers, bricklayers, physical therapists — but also the less usual, such as IBM statistical machine servicemen, electroplaters, foresters, volcanologists.

"Job descriptions, training and qualifications, employment outlook, earnings, and where to write for fuller information are noted. For the trades, it relates hourly wages to geographic locations, and charts the growth and possible future of industries and jobs stemming from them.

"Girls or fellows who plan to go to work immediately upon graduation should look at 'From High School to a Job,' by Paradis. Here are jobs in which one may advance without a BS or BA degree. Banks, telephone companies, insurance firms, large department stores and the government are represented. Many of these companies encourage on-the-job training and even make pos-

sible college attendance for employees with aptitude and ambition.

"The United States government is the largest single employer in the world. But before one can settle down in a 'secure' municipal, state or federal position, a civil service examination must be passed. The Arco Publishing Company puts out hundreds of books to help you plan and study for the government job you want. (Several are held up). Job descriptions and sample tests are given for would-be postal clerks, teachers, plumbers. Ask for the job in which you are interested and we may have it in the 'World of Books' collection.

"If you are one of those lucky individuals who know exactly what they want to do . . . it is quite possible that the library has a special book on your profession, business or trade which will add to your understanding of it.

"Girls who dream of soothing fevered brows and serving humanity in a nurse's uniform, must be sure to read 'A Lamp Is Heavy,' by Sheila Russell. It is a novel about a sheltered child who decides to become a nurse and finds she has a lot to learn about people, life, and love, as well as nursing courses, before she can succeed.

"Here, too, are many commentaries on individual careers, such as 'Invitation to Advertising,' which warns that the clever person with imagination may make money in this field, but the competition is cut-throat; and 'Etiquette in Business,' providing on-the-job help for secretaries and business men, with tips on telephone etiquette, parliamentary procedures, and even how to arrange an office party.

"And now step right over to the college booth for an introduction to what it takes to add a BS or BA to your name."

As a result of that first experiment, the fair became an annual fixture in Baltimore's high schools. The usual procedure was for the Young Adult Services Office to contact the high school librarians and principals through the supervisor of libraries for the Baltimore Department of Education. After blanket approval was obtained a schedule was set up allowing one to three days for each school, depending on enrollment, with all assigned classes visiting the fair for one period each.

Over the years many changes were made as

youth matured earlier and, as the 10th graders seemed a more likely audience than the seniors, the introductory music became modern and popular. The subjects of the individual booths changed. The focus was directed mainly at books and information without benefit of such gimmicks as finger painters and salad chefs, who proved to be more of a distraction than a come-on. The hardbacks gave way to more and more paperbacks. But the "basics" — color, quick, pertinent repartee, often humorous descriptions of booths and books, movement, lists, music, circulating materials — remained the same.

One summer the Young Adult Services Division of the American Library Association adopted the fair pattern for its annual conference. To aid librarians desiring to undertake a similar project

copies of the brochure, "Blueprint for a Book Show," were distributed at the event. The following advice, reflecting notes contained in that pamphlet, bears repeating:

Angels in the Wings

"If the library budget is too slim to cover such items as book booths or special 'World of Books' collections, it is well to remember that service organizations often are looking for worthy educational or social undertakings which they can further. Because the 'World of Books' idea is big, gay and appealing as well as educational, it stands a good chance to win the interest and support of groups such as service clubs, women's clubs, parent-teacher organizations, junior organizations,

VISITORS'-EYE-VIEW *This high school book fair held the rapt attention of students who attended. Members of the staff were on hand to discuss the books exhibited.*

junior associations of commerce, and junior leagues.

"When a librarian goes out to 'catch an angel,' a well-planned approach will increase chances of success.

- Know the purpose of your project.
- In advance, sound out the proper library, school or other authorities to see whether they are in agreement with the ideas and plans formulated.
- Contact a key organization member and ask for a chance to submit the proposal to him.
- Have in hand a list of equipment needed, with approximate costs.
- Also know the approximate number of publications required to present a 'World of Books' in action, and their cost.
- Request an appointment with the governing

board or funding committee. Talk to this group, perhaps at a luncheon meeting. Make good use of facts, enthusiasm, humor and brevity in an all-out attempt to obtain financing for a 'World of Books'.

Booths

- With the drawing shown on page 30 as a guide, any library carpenter or school workshop can turn out a similar booth.
- It is sectional, and therefore transportable. Shudder hinges hold the three sides together. Pegs hold the top of the frame firmly and help secure the counter to the sides.
- The headboard is constructed so that the top sign may be easily slipped into place. It is col-

BALTIMORE HIGH SCHOOL STUDENTS *Gravitated to books of special interest after examining the general collection at the Pratt's book fair.*

lapsible on hinges, and when set up fastened on the back with hook and eye.

- The under trough for duplicate books and related materials is quickly added.
- With little time and trouble amateur seamstresses can design and make draperies and awnings similar to those seen in the illustrations. Fireproof fabric is essential.

Diversified Adaptations

"Every progressive librarian will recognize that the technique used in the book fair is adaptable in whole or in part to other shows and subjects.

- Science carnivals. The large flat counter allows for display of models. Diagrams may be hung against the curtain at the back of a booth, or be attached on the large front board and sides.
- A street carnival which takes the library into the open.
- Demonstrations by cosmeticians, artists and others, featuring refreshments, music, a movie show using a rearview projector, giveaway pamphlets on a variety of subjects, a magazine stand as well as paperback and hardback books, often prove successful. Aided by the color and music, they can draw a crowd to the out-of-doors library scene.
- A library information counter in a shopping district or busy store. The booth may be equipped with telephone connection to other sources of information as well as a ready reference collection, and registration facilities.
- A Christmas gift book show.
- A family program with a booth for each member of a typical family, from pets to great-grandpa.
- An international fair combining books, cookery and handicrafts representing countries and areas of the world. Booths allow for posters, small stoves on the counters, art work, even games with an international flavor.
- A gimmick to publicize library resources at country fairs, park or street festivals, sportsmen's shows, garden shows, pet shows.
- Career day programs. One or more booths can be utilized as slides or videotapes of librarians in action are featured; free pamphlets are distributed; representatives of the profession have a home base from which they reach interested prospects. Of course, this might be expanded to a booth for each profession or job, or type of profession or job.
- Within the library, the large colorful booths dramatize special subjects, such as art, science, black America, black Africa, during special weeks which attempt to play up library materials. Book Week seems particularly appropriate for such treatment.

"Many other uses will appear obvious to librarians who have a flair for creative and effective public relations."

If funds and facilities for special booths are entirely lacking, then any available library tables may be covered with gay cloths, surmounted with suitable books, posters and signs, and used to do a satisfactory promotional job.

Admittedly, book fairs involve hard work and are time-consuming. But when planned and staged with imagination and ingenuity, as a device for stimulating reader-interest, they have few equals.

CHAPTER SEVEN

LIGHTING

Relatively few libraries are equipped with modern lighting for proper presentation of exhibits. Since many library displays have their largest attendance at night, it is often necessary to supplement existing electrical facilities with temporary installations, for more satisfactory viewing by visitors. Sometimes the addition of a few simple spotlights, well-placed, will make a world of difference.

Most power companies provide free advisory service to individuals and agencies seeking help with such problems. But for the benefit of workers who may not have access to the utilities, the following information, provided by G. Wilson Younglove, senior illuminating engineer for the Baltimore Gas and Electric Company, is offered.

Well-planned lighting for a display increases

PROJECTOR AND REFLECTOR LAMPS

Seen here are some of the many inexpensive light sources adaptable for use in either fixed or temporary display arrangements.

(Courtesy Large Lamp Department, General Electric Company, Cleveland, Ohio)

its power to attract attention and makes it easier to examine the items shown. This fact is well-known to supermarket managers, who have found that the same merchandise will sell several times faster to impulse buyers when displayed on a special spotlighted fixture, than it does in its accustomed place on the shelves.

The amount of light which an object reflects determines its visibility. In general, the brightness or quantity of light reflected should be from two to five times that of the surroundings in order to attract attention.

It is a good rule to avoid placing very dark and very light objects near each other if they are equally important to a lighted display. For example, a book jacket in glossy black with bold, wide-stroke blue letters could be very effective, but shown beside pastel-colored jackets would lose effectiveness unless it was spotlighted with many times as much light as its highly reflective associates.

On the market are a variety of inexpensive light sources readily adaptable for use in either fixed or temporary displays. Reflectorized incandescent lamps are available in sizes from 30 watts for small displays, to 500 watt or larger sealed beam lamps with assorted patterns.

The illustration on the preceding page shows some of these. In addition, there is the relatively new 30 watt R 20. Similar in appearance to the 75 watt R 30, but only $3\frac{15}{16}$ inches long and $2\frac{9}{16}$ inches in bulb diameter, this fixture is small enough to be concealed behind the hand. Where concealment of "props" is vital, the advantage is obvious.

The most popular of these lamps have standard screw thread bases and can be used in most adjustable sockets and hoods, a feature which permits their attachment almost anywhere. Others are like automobile headlamps, and require special housing.

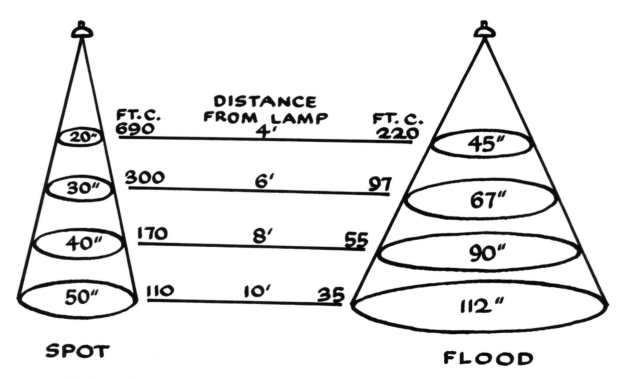

SPOT

FLOOD

PROGRESSIVE LIGHT INTENSITY *Showing maximum amount of light and size of spot for several distances from 150 Watt PAR 38 Lamps. Light intensity at edge will be about ¼ that in center.*

The foregoing chart illustrates the area and light intensity which can be expected at progressive distances from some of the lamps. Since all incandescent illumination produces a considerable amount of infrared energy which upon absorption produces heat, care must be used, particularly with higher wattage lamps placed at close range to fragile books and other valuable items. Heat is extremely harmful to vellum, leather, ivories, painted and illuminated pages.

Because fluorescent lamps produce two to three times as many units of light per watt as do incandescent lamps, they often are preferred in show cases or other confined spaces where heat presents a problem. However, the light from fluorescent tubes cannot be controlled as can that from filament lamps, and they are therefore more frequently used for general area lighting, rather than for accenting. There is, however, a reflectorized fluorescent lamp available in either 40 inch or 96 inch length, which is satisfactory for lighting show cases, wall cases, shelf displays, and similar areas, since about 60 per cent more light is emitted from one side of the tube than from the other (see over).

When colors of the materials on display are important, it becomes necessary to use discretion in the selection of light sources. Incandescent light, which practically all people are accustomed to and accept, produces all colors in a continuous spectrum, but has a preponderance of yellow. With fluorescent lamps, however, the color of the light emitted is dependent on the combination of powdered chemical phosphors used to coat the inside of the tube. Since all presently known phosphors which emit red radiation are relatively low in efficiency, and since the early research in fluoresecent lamps rather naturally sought maximum efficiencies, most of the tubes were lacking in red radiation.

For this reason color rendition was poor in the early fluorescent tubes, with all of the yellow-orange-red tones distorted and grayed. A "soft white" tube was then developed, particularly for use in the display of red meats, butter, produce and other foods, which had been hitherto unacceptable to buyers because of the greenish-gray appearance that they took on under the early fluorescent tubes. However, "soft white" has a pinkish cast, and is therefore limited in its application.

Accordingly, two deluxe tubes have been introduced which, although somewhat lower in efficiency, produce either a warm white or a cool white light, as the result of the addition of enough red to give good color rendition. Together with standard warm white and cool white, they cover practically all display requirements.

In wall cases or for lighting objects displayed on shelves where it is necessary to keep the cross-section of light to a minimum in order to avoid obscuring displays, there are fluorescent show case channels just large enough to support the sockets and carry the necessary wires — approximately 1 x 2 inches, including the fluorescent tube. Under such circumstances the bulky ballast, an essential part of the circuit of all lamps depending on an electric arc, is remotely located in the base of the case or in an adjoining room. This is especially advantageous in libraries where ballast noise could be annoying.

When arranging lighting for a display, either incandescent or fluorescent, it is essential that the source of light be located for best treatment of surfaces to be observed both from a distance and at close range. Here the exhibits worker with a knowledge of stage lighting techniques has a valuable aid, for just as spotlights from the auditorium, and border lights, and spots overhead and behind the proscenium arch provide excellent vertical and horizontal illumination for a theatrical production, so, too, do they for displays.

If the exhibit includes highly polished material, it is only necessary to remember the law of optics which states that the angle of the reflected ray will be equal to the angle of the ray of light striking the surface from a normal to the reflecting surface (next drawing).

Lighting show windows represents a particularly difficult problem because of the reflection in the plate glass of buildings across the way,

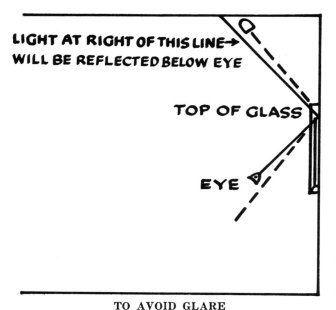

as well as of the cars and people on the street. It is extremely difficult to compete with illumination values of from 5,000 to 10,000 foot candles outside the window. The lighter the display background, the less disturbing the reflections will be. With open back windows and interior illumination of 50 to 100 foot candles, which is extremely good, the problem

is still difficult. With interior illumination of 5 foot candles or less, quite common in older buildings, show window reflections cannot be overcome except by the extensive use of large areas of highly reflective vertical background materials to compete with the high outside light levels.

Fluorescent lighting can be used to provide these high background brightnesses, but incandescent spotlighting is more effective for lighting the display itself, because spot beams can provide highlights, accents and interest which the flat lighting of fluorescent tubing cannot do. On occasion the real attraction value of a display may depend on highlights and shadows, light patterns, centers of focus, textures and color.

Interior displays offer infinite variety and challenge to the ingenuity of the exhibitor. A reflectorized lamp in a gaily-painted fruit juice can, with due regard for safety and fire protection requirements, can make the difference between a book on a shelf and an interest-compelling display. The chart below indicates what can be done with a 4 foot asymmetric fluorescent light strip, with the light bracketed at various distances from the vertical display panel. This is particularly applicable to dis-

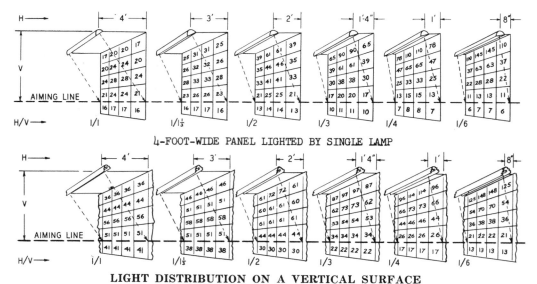

LIGHT DISTRIBUTION ON A VERTICAL SURFACE
Indicating probable effects of a 4 foot fluorescent light strip on a bulletin board type display.
(*Courtesy Large Lamp Department, General Electric Company, Cleveland, Ohio*)

plays of such materials as maps, pamphlets and photographs. The chart shows the degree of uniformity of light distribution which can reasonably be expected.

Glass display cases present another problem which can be handled by mounting the light source in or on the upper front edge. A conventional show case fixture for fluorescent tubes is best suited. However, the reflectorized fluorescent lamp mentioned earlier can be used, and an extremely low-cost incandescent lamp known as T 10 RFL, available in 25 watt and 40 watt sizes, frequently does a good job. This is a filament lamp about 6 inches long, inserted and silver-coated on half the tubular envelope. in a T or tubular bulb, 1¼ inches in diameter. Mounted in a porcelain medium base socket, it provides the display worker with a wide variety of interesting applications. Aluminum foil also makes a good reflector. With a little ingenuity and a few cents, the display worker can sometimes create lighting miracles.

In the matter of rare or fragile books and objects, great care must be exercised to provide a safe environment. There is probably no greater authority on this subject than the United States Bureau of Standards, whose per-

sonnel have studied all factors affecting the preservation of such priceless documents as the Constitution and the Declaration of Independence. They report greater damage caused by blue light in the spectrum than by the red. The relative probable rate of damage from lighting of equal intensity is given:

Zenith sky light	100
Overcast sky	31.7
Sunlight	16.5
Fluorescent	
Cool white deluxe	11.5
Warm white deluxe	9.2
Incandescent	2.8

Glass and plastic filters are available to reduce the rate of damage, most of which involves fading or discoloration, brittleness or disintegration. Information on their effectiveness can be obtained from the Bureau of Standards, Washington 25, D.C.

By using imagination and inventiveness, library workers can meet almost any lighting challenge, with the result that many a dull-looking, difficult-to-view exhibit will be transformed into an effective instrument for the dissemination of knowledge.

INTERIOR CASE LIGHTING

Good lighting adds immeasurably to the value of exhibits. But problems of glare and light diffusion inside glass cases are often difficult to overcome. The Free Library of Philadelphia has found this type satisfactory.

EXTERIOR CASE LIGHTING

In areas where library lighting is poor, standard fluorescent light fixtures make displays more meaningful to visitors.

41

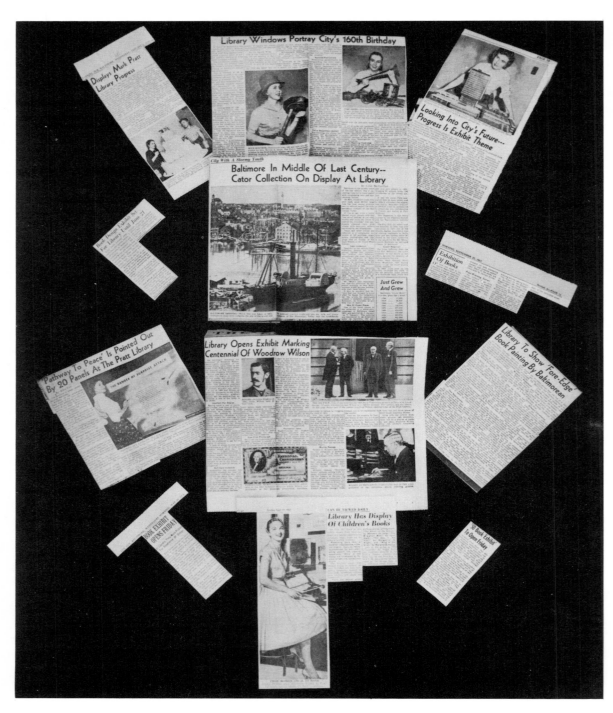

PRESS PROMOTION *Library displays may be covered at length in news stories, illustrated features and special columns. In addition, they should be listed briefly, whenever possible, in calendars of events and art gallery exhibits notices.*

CHAPTER EIGHT

PROMOTION IS A "MUST"

Preparing an exhibit is only part of the job. One must also promote it. For what advantage is there in setting up an effective, informative display if it is seen only by a relatively few people and only those few are stimulated by it to do additional reading?

Therefore, the librarian must reach out into the community through all available means — newspapers, television, radio, church bulletins, farm and labor publications, house organs, school papers and others affording free coverage — to announce the event and report some of its more interesting features.

The press publicity should start as soon as plans for the show are well in hand. Brief at first, the releases should lengthen as the opening date approaches, until the buildup reaches its climax with the actual "unveiling."

Notwithstanding the gains of television and radio media in recent years, newspaper publicity remains an important type of promotion for libraries.

Stories should always be written from the reader's, rather than from the library's, point of view. Follow as closely as possible the style of the newspapers to which the items are submitted.

ATTRACTIVE "BAIT" *A pretty girl always adds interest to newspaper photographs calling attention to library displays.* (Courtesy The Baltimore Sunday American)

Here are a few elementary rules of journalism:

1. Type story on plain white paper, 8½ x 11 inches, double or triple-spaced, one side only. The typescript must be sharp and clear.

2. In upper left-hand corner put the sender's name, address and telephone number, so that the editor or his aide can verify or expand copy forwarded with minimum effort.

3. If at any time a special release date is desired, put FOR RELEASE ON ...., 19........ (exact date) in upper right-hand corner of Page 1.

4. Start copy one-third down on the page, leaving wide margins and indentations.

5. Use simple words, short sentences and paragraphs.

6. Do not hyphenate words at end of line, but place on next line when space is insufficient for completion.

7. Check facts, names, initials and titles carefully, to insure accuracy.

8. Give all pertinent information (answering the reporter's Five W's — Who, What, Why, When and Where) in the first paragraph, elaborating in subsequent paragraphs.

9. When release runs to more than one page, write (more) at lower right of each sheet of continuation.

10. Indicate article's end by placing number symbol # (single or multiple) several spaces below the final paragraph, center.

Copy to the various other publications should go out well in time for the editors' deadlines, ascertained in advance.

In connection with exhibits more elaborate and ambitious than usual, related posters may be distributed for placement in the windows or interiors of drugstores, groceries, restaurants, laundries, fire houses and similar establishments.

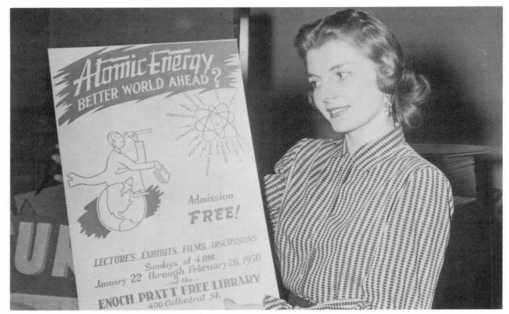

POSTER PROMOTION — *Make the most of this good public relations tool. Posters produced in quantity are valuable for spreading the word about the library's more ambitious shows. Recommended sizes are 9 × 20 inches, 14 × 20 inches and 17 × 22 inches, depending upon individual preference. However, the larger posters are sometimes difficult to place because of space considerations.*

Items for store windows and counter display should have cardboard easels attached. Boy Scouts and other youth groups are often willing to deliver the posters, but the original contacts should be made by the librarian.

Letters calling attention to the event may be directed to the presidents of organizations for announcement at meetings, and book marks or fliers may be distributed from supermarkets, shopping centers, banks, skating rinks, and other places frequented by large numbers of people.

Information intended for radio and television, short and to the point, should reach program directors two weeks or ten days before the exhibit starts. At the Enoch Pratt Free Library it is the practice to send a group of spot announcements, ranging in length from 25 to 125 words, to all local stations. These can be used in breaks between programs at any hour of the day or night, and are difficult for listeners to escape. Therefore, they are more effective than ordinary full-length library programs, which have a limited audience and are up against stiff commercial competition.

(Of course, it is also desirable whenever possible for the librarian to make guest appearances on well-established, popular programs. In this way the exhibits message can be additionally projected.)

If there is no early display deadline set, preface each spot announcement with the line: **SPOT ANNOUNCEMENT FOR ANY CONVENIENT TIME.**

When a given period for broadcasting is desired, specify it:
SPOT ANNOUNCEMENT FOR JUNE 18, 19 AND 20, 19....

Type and capitalize all copy, double or triple-space, using plain white paper, 8½ x 11 inches, one side only. In the upper left-hand corner note your name, library address and telephone number, for quick identification and reference.

Learn the wishes of your local stations. Some prefer original copies of individual "spots" on separate sheets of paper. Others will take several announcements on a single sheet, originals or carbons. It goes without saying that all carbon copies must be distinct and legible. When composing the "spots," vary your phraseology, even though repeating the basic information.

Following are a few radio and television examples associated with Baltimore exhibits projects in past years:

SPOT ANNOUNCEMENT FOR ANY CONVENIENT TIME, NOVEMBER 20 — DECEMBER 22.

IT'S CHRISTMAS FAIRYLAND TIME AT THE ENOCH PRATT FREE LIBRARY. ENJOY THE DELIGHTFUL CHRISTMAS BOOK SHOW AT THE LIBRARY'S MAIN BUILDING, DAILY EXCEPT SUNDAY, THROUGH DECEMBER 26.

SPOT ANNOUNCEMENT FOR WEDNESDAY, THURSDAY, FRIDAY, SATURDAY (NOVEMBER 14, 15, 16, 17)

HAVE YOU A BOOK GIFT PROBLEM? THEN BE SURE TO VISIT THE ENOCH PRATT FREE LIBRARY'S CHRISTMAS BOOK SHOW, OPENING MONDAY AT THE LIBRARY'S MAIN BUILDING, 400 CATHEDRAL STREET. IN GAY CARNIVAL ATMOSPHERE YOU MAY LOOK OVER BOOKS FOR ALL AGES AND READING TASTES — BOOKS TO SUIT EVERY PURSE AND PURPOSE.

SPOT ANNOUNCEMENT FOR WEDNESDAY, THURSDAY, FRIDAY, SATURDAY (NOVEMBER 14, 15, 16, 17)

DON'T MISS THE ENOCH PRATT FREE LIBRARY'S CHRISTMAS BOOK SHOW, STARTING MONDAY AT THE MAIN BUILDING, CATHEDRAL AND FRANKLIN STREETS. ENJOY THE JOLLY SANTA CLAUS DECORATIONS, THE COLORFUL BOOK BOOTHS, AND OTHER ATTRACTIVE FEATURES. LET TRAINED SPECIALISTS SOLVE YOUR PERSONAL BOOK GIFT PROBLEMS. THE PRATT LIBRARY'S CHRISTMAS BOOK SHOW WILL BE OPEN FROM 9 A.M. TO 9 P.M. DAILY EXCEPT SUNDAYS AND HOLIDAYS THROUGH DECEMBER 26.

SPOT ANNOUNCEMENT FOR USE NOW THROUGH MARCH 24.

IMPORTANT BOOKS OF THE TWENTIETH CENTURY, INCLUDING THE FAVORITES OF PROMINENT BALTIMOREANS, WILL GO ON DISPLAY TUESDAY, MARCH 25 IN THE PRATT LIBRARY. HOW MANY HAVE YOU READ? HOW MANY HAVE YOU MISSED? VISIT THE PRATT'S CENTRAL BUILDING AND RENEW ACQUAINTANCE WITH THESE BOOKS WHICH ARE PART OF AMERICA'S HERITAGE.

SPOT ANNOUNCEMENT FOR USE MARCH 25 AND AFTER

MEMORABLE YEARS — 1901 to 1950! YEARS OF WAR AND PEACE, BREADLINES, BOOMS AND STARTLING HEADLINES. WHAT BOOKS HAVE AMERICANS READ DURING THESE EVENTFUL TIMES? VISIT THE PRATT LIBRARY'S EXHIBITION OF NOTABLE BOOKS OF THE LAST HALF-CENTURY, AND SEE FOR YOURSELF. THE SHOW WILL REMAIN THROUGH MAY 17. LIBRARY HOURS ARE 9 A.M. TO 9 P.M. DAILY EXCEPT SUNDAY.

SPOT ANNOUNCEMENT FOR USE MARCH 25 AND AFTER

REMEMBER WHEN F. SCOTT FITZGERALD WAS THE RAGE AND SINCLAIR LEWIS'S "MAIN STREET" CAUSED A FUROR? THE TWENTIETH CENTURY IS RICH IN MEMORABLE BOOKS AND THE ENOCH PRATT FREE LIBRARY NOW HAS ON DISPLAY A SPECIAL EXHIBIT OF BOOKS OF THE HALF CENTURY FROM 1901 to 1950. BE SURE TO SEE IT. ENJOY SOME OF THE FAMOUS TITLES OF THOSE TIMES.

CHAPTER NINE

BASIC SILK SCREEN

When a library bond issue or some other major project requiring all-out publicity is pending, the silk screen process is excellent for producing display posters and signs in quantity for community-wide distribution.

Conducted somewhat on the printing press principle, but operated manually by small, non-commercial agencies, the silk screen is both time and labor-saving, particularly for medium-sized and larger libraries with the necessary staff.

Essential equipment and materials are as follows:

Silk screen film
Film-stencil knife
Clear gummed tape
Masking tape
12 XX silk screen
  stencil silk, meshes
  124 per inch
Adhering solution
Silk screen paint
  solvent
Lacquer thinner
Silk screen paints
Squeegee
¼ inch plywood

Glue
Metal hinges (two)
Stapling gun with
  staples
Cardboard (or
  paper) of desired
  thickness
Brown wrapping
  paper
Work table or bench
White cloths
Printing frame (or
  four 2 x 4's)

SILK SCREEN FRAME *This frame, or box, is large enough to take a full sheet of cardboard, 28 x 44 inches. Because of its size, making hand-manipulation of long runs tiring, a pulley device was attached, to help carry the weight during the raising and lowering process. Pulley ropes have here been temporarily disconnected. Note the "window" with film design on the silk exposed, ready to receive the paint.*

A simple silk screen printing frame or box can be purchased or made inexpensively. To build one, determine the largest size poster or sign you are likely to need in quantity, and allow a four-inch margin all around. Accordingly, if your biggest poster is to be 22 by 28 inches, saw two 2 by 4's to a length of 26 inches, and another pair to a length of 32 inches. Nail the pieces together or, better still, groove the joints, gluing the edges. The latter method is preferable, because the frame must be rigid in construction for precise registry.

Lay the silk on the frame, with the edges overlapping; stretch at both ends and staple overhanging edges tightly all around, so there are no sags or distortions. When this is done wet the silk thoroughly, then let dry. This draws the silk taut, as it must be, for satisfactory performance. Next cover the stapled areas and sides of the box with several layers of two-inch masking tape, to keep them smooth and neat. The frame is now finished.

Set a piece of quarter-inch plywood a few inches larger than the frame on a rough table or bench, the front edges parallel, and nail the plywood on its face. Then with two sturdy metal hinges attach the box securely to the rear section of the plywood. This will keep it in place and give accurate register.

Regardless of the color chosen for any single-paint job to be reproduced, the original pattern should be black on white, which is easiest to see under the film.

Let us say that the projected poster will measure 17 x 22 inches.

Silk screen film is a lacquer film made of two layers (the bottom layer is a supporting sheet of wax paper) manufactured in rolls 300 by 40 inches, or it may be purchased by the yard. Cut a piece 19 x 24 inches for the job at hand, and place over the poster pattern lacquer side up. The lettering and design are plainly visible.

Using the stencil knife, trace lightly along the outline of letters and art work with just enough pressure to cut upper surface, then peel off the portions of the lacquer film encompassed. Be careful not to damage the paper beneath. When the cutting is complete, the job is ready to apply to the silk. This is the most difficult part of the operation, and success hinges on how it comes out.

CUTTING THE STENCIL

The sharp point of the stencil knife moves lightly along the outline of the letters and illustrations on the pattern below. This is a delicate operation, and just enough pressure should be used to pierce the upper surface, without damage to the wax paper base. Then the lacquer film within the cut area is peeled off, after which the job is ready to apply to the silk.

Proceed with caution. Take the sample poster (over which the film was cut) and with four small pieces of gummed transparent tape at corners affix it to the plywood board under the frame. Then place the film over the poster so that the cutout letters and design are superimposed exactly over the original work, and tape this at corners. Avoid excessive use of tape, as too much may tear the fabric later.

Lower the box or frame, resting it on the plywood base, in preparation for transferring the pattern to the silk. Take two good-sized pieces of clean white cloth, one for applying the adhering solution and the other for wiping dry. (The adhering solution, packaged in metal cans, is highly inflammable. Be sure to enforce NO SMOKING regulations not only during the operation, but also until the leftovers are safely disposed of.)

Saturate one cloth, squeezing off the excess liquid. With that in one hand and the dry cloth in the other, you are ready to begin. Take the wet cloth and with long, sweeping strokes, moisten the entire film area. As soon as this has been accomplished, repeat the action with the dry cloth. This is important, as the adhering solution dissolves the film into the silk.

An excess of wetness will make the penetration too deep, ruining the stencil. On the other hand, if the cloth is not wet enough, the film will not adhere properly to the silk, and the results will be disappointing. If possible, experiment with a few small pieces of film in advance, until the proper technique is mastered.

When the film has adhered to the silk, let it dry for about five minutes. The adhering liquid evaporates very quickly. During this time raise the frame, and with a pencil draw two lines along the left side and top of the sample poster. Then take two narrow cardboard strips and lay them against the pencil lines, facing out. Tape, tack or staple them carefully into position. The angle-like arrangement will serve as guide lines.

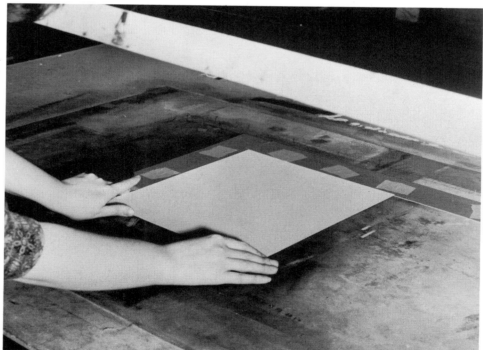

INSERTING THE POSTER BOARD *Top and left edges must be placed flush against the cardboard guideline strips for exact registry, otherwise the printing will be off balance. Speed is imperative, as silk screen paints dry rapidly. As each poster is imprinted it is withdrawn and a new card slipped into position, without waste of time or motion.*

By this time the film should be dry. Peel off the wax paper backing. If the film has adhered properly, the paper will strip off cleanly. Should any part of the film be removed with the paper, replace the latter, drop the box, and with the damp cloth rub the part in question lightly until it has adhered, then remove the paper entirely.

At this point take a piece of brown wrapping paper slightly larger than the box. Cut from it a section extending just a little beyond the film area, then affix the paper to the frame with only the cut-out or "window" section of the silk exposed.

Attach the brown paper to the sides of the box with short strips of masking tape, and use a double thickness of the tape around the edge of the "window" opening. Make sure the tape is down tight and smooth, so that no paint can seep through. The screen is then ready to run.

The correct number of poster cards, all measured meticulously and of uniform size, should be at hand on a nearby table or book truck, where they may be picked up quickly, one by one. It is wise to have a few more than the number needed, as insurance against spoilage. Commercial houses generally allow 10 per cent for poor impressions, but the Enoch Pratt Free Library seldom has more than one or two to a job, even when hundreds of copies are involved.

For the "dry run," or preliminary testing, the Pratt uses old newspaper pages. In that way, if an imperfection appears, it can be corrected without waste of cardboard.

Silk screen paints are obtainable in a variety of colors, but the supplier will provide instructions for mixing special shades when desired. Stir paint well. If too thick, add silk screen

OPERATION SQUEEGEE

A small quantity of silk screen paint of the desired color is poured from the can to the right of the "window," the full length of the film. Then the exhibits worker, holding the wooden handle of the squeegee, with the rubber blade pushes the paint firmly across the film. This transfers the pattern to the card below.

50

"CLOTHESLINE" DRYERS *Overhead wires strung from wall to wall, with metal clips attached, can accommodate a large run of freshly silk-screened items without cluttering regular work space.*

paint solvent. The solvent is used also for cleaning up the paint after the job is done, and lacquer thinner removes the stencil from silk.

When paint is at proper consistency, make sure that the first card is in the correct position under the frame, inserted against the guide-line strips. Place newspaper over this, and lower frame. Pour a small quantity of paint from the can to the right of the "window," the full length of the film. Next take the squeegee (the tool which forces the paint through the silk) and, holding the wooden handle, push the rubber blade firmly across the film. Raise the box, remove the newspaper, and check to see that the paint has come through evenly, giving the letters and illustration a sharp, clean line.

If all is well begin to run the cards, squeegee-ing paint back and forth, raising and lowering frame as required, removing screened card each time and placing a fresh card in position until the work is completed. Add more paint as needed. If the letters are light and not fully coated at times, the paint is too thick. Conversely, if paint spreads too fast, it is too thin.

Imprinted cards, when wet, can be stacked standing around the room to dry. The Pratt Library has three long overhead wires strung like clotheslines, wall to wall in the Exhibits Workoom, with metal clips attached. This allows suspension of several hundred posters or signs simultaneously, without cluttering up the regular work space. For best results silk screen items should dry overnight.

51

SILK SCREEN STACKING *When no drying racks are available, posters may be placed against each other in the manner of building a house of cards. However, care must be exercised, or the whole arrangement will collapse.*

If the budget permits, multicolor jobs can be produced. Cut a separate film for each color. Before starting a new run make sure the cleanup of the preceding run has been thorough, and the register properly adjusted. The printing register must be perfect every time, as over-lapping or inaccurate placement will ruin the work. Whenever possible do silk screening in dry weather, as dampness may add to operational difficulties.

NOTE: For special problems and advice, consult your graphic arts supplier.

DIVERSIFIED DISPLAY SUGGESTIONS

Library exhibits may relate to any idea or subject tying in with materials in the library's collection.

Many of the displays pictured in the following pages are shown through courtesy of Miss Howard Hubbard, gracious and capable chief of public relations at the Enoch Pratt Free Library, in Baltimore. Designed and executed under her supervision by the talented artists on her staff at various times during the past decade — William J. Bond, Charles J. Cipolloni, Frank J. Cipolloni, Aileen W. Cipolloni and Emily H. Hagan — they were photographed by William H. Ochs, of the Sussman-Ochs Company.

MAN: HIS FIRST MILLION YEARS

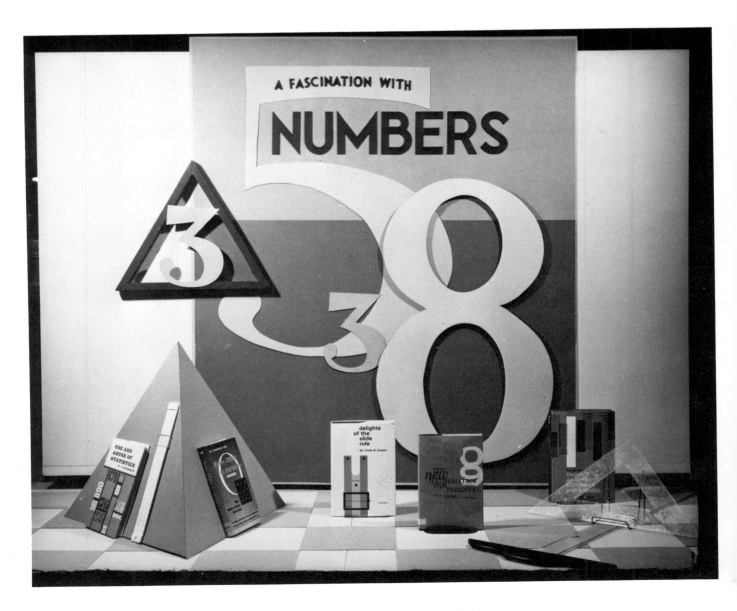

A FASCINATION WITH NUMBERS

CHINA: PAST AND PRESENT

LANGUAGE BOOKS AND READING

NOTABLE BOOKS

GREAT BOOKS DISCUSSION GROUPS

I ALWAYS MEANT TO READ THAT

GREAT DECISIONS

PRATT LIBRARY LOAN

NEXT QUESTION?

THE PLAY'S THE THING

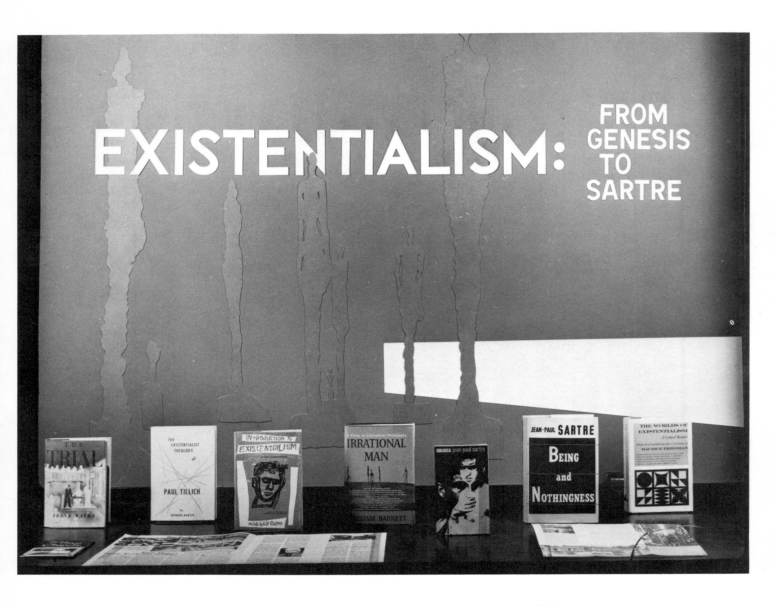

EXISTENTIALISM: FROM GENESIS TO SARTRE

BROWSER'S WELCOME TO FINE ARTS

PERENNIAL FAVORITES

COLORFUL CUTOUTS

The figurines shown on these pages were originally taken from travel posters. They were salvaged when the poster edges became tattered.

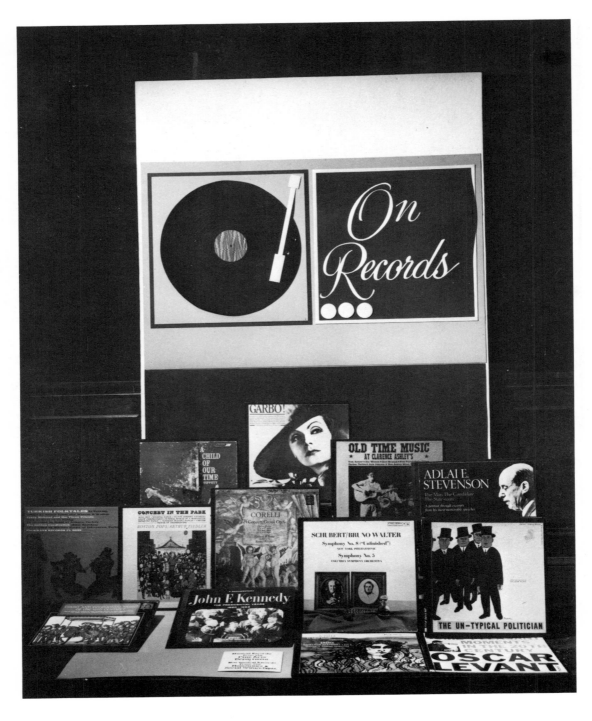

RECORDINGS

MAP-MINDED?

INDIAN ART OF LATIN AMERICA

PRESIDENTS

UNITED STATES CENSUS OF 1970

FEDERAL INCOME TAX

FEDERAL INCOME TAX

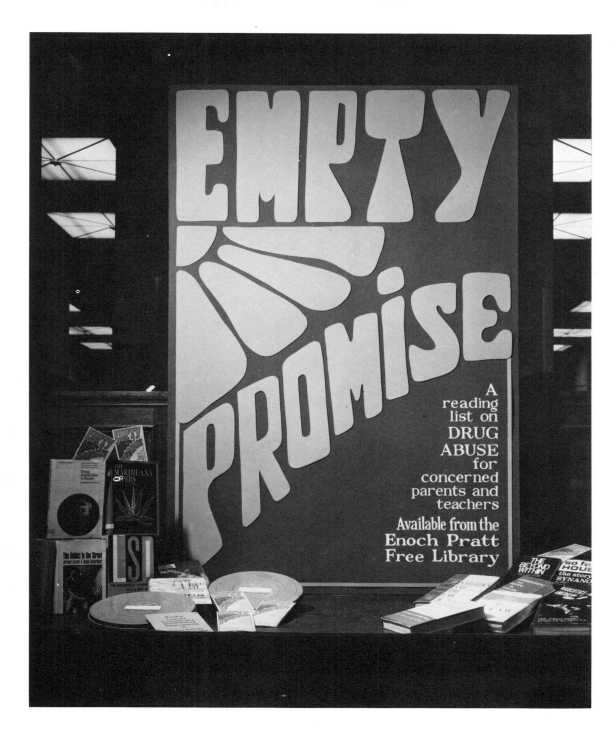

EMPTY PROMISE (A reading list on drug abuse)

IMPURITIES IN THE AIR

ENERGY: PROBLEMS AND PROMISES

EARTH DAY

BOOK WEEK

BOOK POWER (Children's Book Week)

THE NEWBERY — CALDECOTT MEDALS

TO OUTER SPACE WITH CHILDREN'S BOOKS

BOOKS FOR THE CHILD IN TODAY'S WORLD

ECOLOGY AND OTHER NEW SUBJECTS

OUTER SPACE AND FAR OUT ENCHANTMENTS

STORIES TO TELL

BOOKS FOR THE FUN OF READING
(Along with school books)

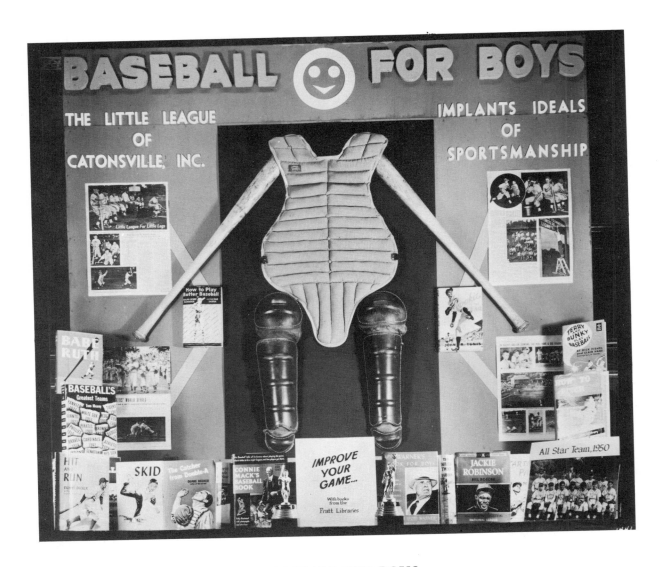

BASEBALL FOR BOYS

INDIANS

THE 100TH BIRTHDAY OF ALICE IN WONDERLAND

POETRY FOR THE YOUNG

CHILDREN'S BOOKS FOR VALENTINE'S DAY

CHILDREN'S BOOKS FOR VALENTINE'S DAY

PRINTING WEEK

LENTEN READING

LENTEN READING

INTER-FAITH COOPERATION

SEED CATALOG TIME

BORROWED IDEA

The eye-catching center decoration is a cardboard enlargement of the magazine cover appearing to left and right.

NATIONAL MUSIC WEEK

ARMED FORCES WEEK

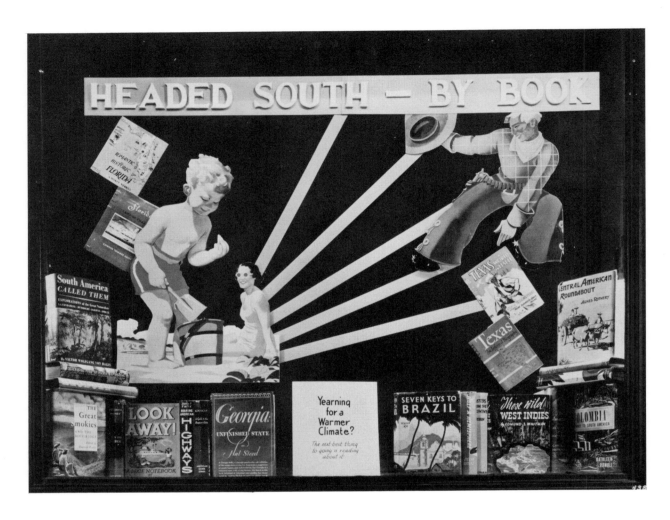

HEADED SOUTH — BY BOOK

RE-USING MATERIAL *As these opposite pages indicate, display decorations may be repeated if the arrangement varies. The backdrop illustrations were cut from travel posters which had outlived their usefulness.*

CHILDREN'S BOOKS FOR A SUMMER'S DAY

PREPARED FOR TRAVEL

GO PLACES WITH BOOKS

GO PLACES WITH BOOKS

AMERICA AT WAR, 1775-1783

A DAY TO REMEMBER — JULY 4, 1776

THE UNITED STATES SINCE JULY 4, 1776

BIRDS ON THE AIR

ANIMAL ADVENTURES

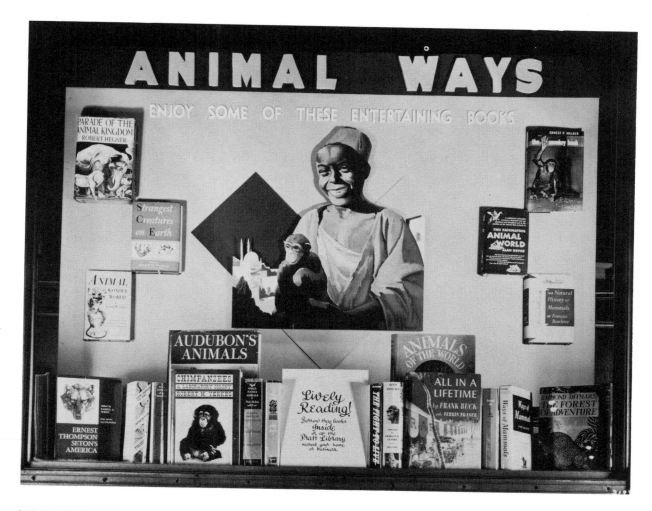

TREATMENT CAN BE VARIED

While subjects may be repeated from time to time, the displays should be handled differently. The illustrations on both backdrops presented here are commercial poster cutouts.

SURFING

SUMMER SPORTS

LABOR DAY

DEFENDERS' DAY

AMERICAN ART WEEK

120

UNITED NATIONS

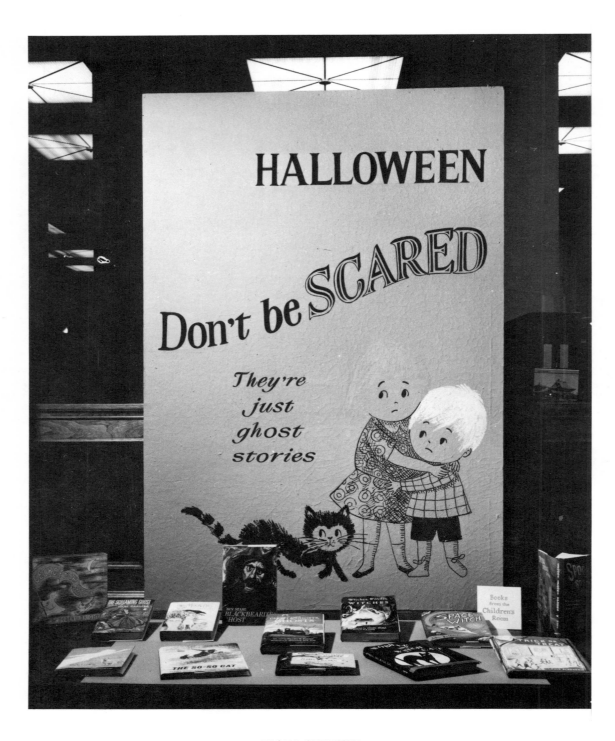

HALLOWEEN

122

THANKSGIVING

CHRISTMAS SEALS

GIVE THE OLD FAVORITES

BASIC ICE SKATING SKILLS

SKIING WEATHER

WOMEN'S LIB

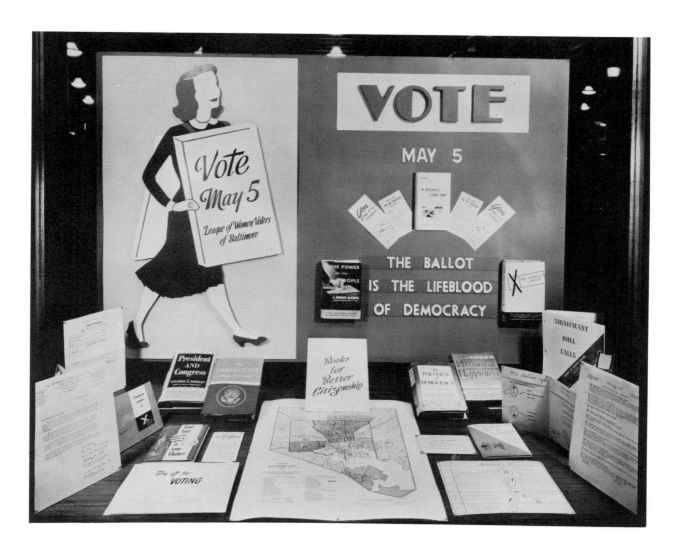

VOTE

40+ EMPLOYMENT

ON THE HUMOROUS SIDE

ALL ABOUT THE WEATHER

MILK

STRETCH THAT DOLLAR

AFRO-AMERICAN CLEAN BLOCK CAMPAIGN

JOIN THE YMCA — JOIN THE LIBRARY, TOO

CANCER CONTROL MONTH

MENTAL HEALTH

SAVE YOUR VISION WEEK

NATIONAL NEWSPAPER WEEK

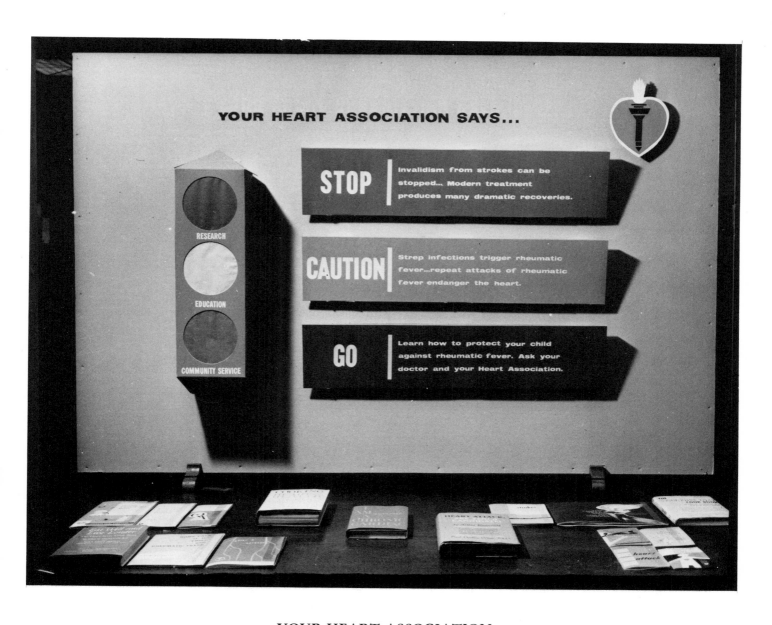

YOUR HEART ASSOCIATION

THE MARYLAND HISTORICAL SOCIETY

APPENDIX

CATCHY CAPTIONS

To attract attention, display "headlines" must have instantaneous appeal for readers. Brevity is desirable. Alliteration is often effective, but should not be overdone.

The main caption is designed to give a clue to the exhibit's general coverage. It is well to add a supplementary line, too, pointing up the book content. Here are a few examples from the Enoch Pratt Free Library:

THE MONEY MARKET
Causes and Effects of Currency Changes

STRETCH THAT DOLLAR
Books Can Help Beat the High Cost of Living

MIND OVER MATTER
Human Behavior Makes Interesting Reading

WOMEN IN TODAY'S WORLD
Varied Views of the Feminine Role in Modern Life

TO THE LADIES!
Books That Enhance Feminine Attractiveness
and Charm

LIFE'S LIGHTER SIDE
Enjoy Some of the Library's Wit-and-Humor
Volumes

THIS GOOD EARTH
Let's Safeguard Our Natural Resources

PERENNIAL FAVORITES
Books That Have Stood the Test of Time

LONG, LONG AGO
Stories of Other Days and Ways

BOOKS FOR THE WHOLE FAMILY
Good Reading for the Longer Evenings Ahead

PLANNING A PARTY?
Assure Its Success with Library Books

WORLD COOKERY
Try a Few Dishes That Are Different,
with the Help of These Books

ARM-CHAIR TRAVEL
Tour the Country with These
Entertaining Books

BOOK TONIC
A Sure Cure for Spring Fever

OTHER CAPTION SUGGESTIONS:

MEET THE AUTHORS
BOOKS FOR LAZY DAYS
INDIAN TALES AND TRAILS
"BLESSED EVENT" BOOKS
BUILD YOUR BUSINESS WITH BOOKS
BROTHERHOOD...PATTERN FOR PEACE
THE GREAT AND NEAR-GREAT
HERE'S HOUSING
OUR AMERICAN HERITAGE
A TREASURE CHEST OF CHILDREN'S STORIES
ROSES ARE READ
KEEP ON LEARNING
BOOKS THAT BOYS LIKE
FIGHT INFLATION
PET PROBLEMS!
HAPPY MOTORING!
ADVENTURES IN SCIENCE
COLLECTOR'S LUCK
DRUG DISCOVERIES
VACATION READING
THE EMPLOYMENT PICTURE
POINTERS ON PLASTICS

ONCE UPON A TIME...
BIRD NEIGHBORS
HOLIDAYS AHEAD
READ 'EM, COWBOY
GO PLACES WITH BOOKS
THE MAGIC OF MAPS
READING FOR FUN
SPRINGTIME IS READING TIME
HELPS FOR HOMEMAKERS
BOOKS IN SEARCH OF CHILDREN
WINTER WANDERINGS
CHILDREN'S ROOM "SPECIALS"
BOOK FARE FOR THE FOURTH
WEATHER OR NO...
TODAY'S CHILDREN
AMERICA'S STORY
CANADA BOUND — BY BOOK
EXPLORERS ALL!
HORSE AND BUGGY DAYS
THE LAND OF MAKE-BELIEVE
COOL READING FOR WARM DAYS
MOUNTAIN MAGIC

If You Want to Mix Your Own Paints . . .

Red + Yellow	= **Orange**
Yellow + Blue	= **Green**
Blue + Red	= **Purple**
Purple + White	= **Lavender**
Blue + White	= **Powder Blue**
Red + White	= **Pink**
Black + White	= **Grey**
Orange + Purple	= **Brown**
Brown + White	= **Tan**
Brown + Red	= **Terracotta**
Orange + Red	= **Tangerine**
Yellow + Orange	= **Golden Yellow**
Red + Purple	= **Turkey Red**
Black + Blue	= **Navy Blue**
Blue + Green	= **Turquoise**
Green + Yellow	= **Jade Green**
Green + Small Amount Black	= **Forest Green**

To make a color lighter add white

To make a color duller and darker add black, or:

A trace of Green will dull Red	A trace of Red will dull Green
" " Yellow " " Purple	" " Purple " " Yellow
" " Orange " " Blue	" " Blue " " Orange

NOTE: In combining paints, use small amounts at a time, and stir well after each addition.

When matching colors, it is advisable to let a small sample of the mixed paint dry thoroughly for best comparison. Tones have a tendency to lighten in the drying process.

POSSIBLE SOURCES OF FREE AND INEXPENSIVE DISPLAY MATERIALS

Part I

Listed below are firms and agencies which in the past have been known to distribute posters, charts, prints, maps, directories, booklets or pamphlets without charge or at relatively low cost. (Readers may also wish to consult "Free and Inexpensive Learning Materials," published by the George Peabody College for Teachers). No prices are given for salable items because these may change intermittently. With the passage of time, also, stocks frequently become depleted or are discontinued. Therefore, when planning to obtain any particular item or items, prospective users are cautioned to contact the company involved to ascertain availability and price, if any. While the supply of free materials lasts, their sponsors will generally send one copy on request. Use professional addresses wherever possible.

ABC School Supply, Inc.
437 Armour Circle, N.E.
Atlanta, Ga. 30324
Gummed decorations, prints, cut-out and pin-up letters, felt doll kits, etc.

Abbott Laboratories, Public Relations Dept.
Abbott Park
North Chicago, Ill. 60064
Chart showing how spores and molds are converted to antibiotics.

Aetna Life and Casualty Co.
Information and Education Dept. D-A
151 Farmington Avenue
Hartford, Conn. 06105
Posters featuring traffic safety and fire prevention.

Allied Chemical Corp. Public Relations Dept.
1411 Broadway
New York, N.Y. 10018
Chart showing natural and synthetic products derived from coal.

American Association for Health, Physical Education and Recreation
1201 16th Street, N.W.
Washington, D.C. 20036
Charts dealing with basketball, volley ball and other sports.

American Classical League, Service Bureau
Miami University
Oxford, Ohio 45056
Large posters in color, for possible use in displays related to Greek and Roman history, Latin, mythology and similar subjects.

American Dental Association
211 E. Chicago Avenue
Chicago, Ill. 60611
Color charts illustrating the development of human teeth, the process of enamel decay, and the care of teeth.

American Forest Products Industries, Inc.
1816 N Street, N.W.
Washington, D.C. 20036
Map showing forests and trees of the United States; charts illustrating growth of a tree and products of the tree farm.

American Heart Association
44 E. 23rd Street
New York, N.Y. 10010
Posters concerning the heart, its function and care.

American Institute of Baking,
Consumer Service Dept.
400 E. Ontario Street
Chicago, Ill. 60611
Posters, charts and booklets related to nutrition and health.

American Insurance Association
85 John Street
New York, N.Y. 10038
Posters pointing up fire prevention.

American Map Co.
3 W. 61st Street
New York, N.Y. 10023
Map of Story Land.

American Museum of Natural History
  American Museum Shop
    Central Park West and 79th Street
    New York, N.Y. 10024
        Maps and charts bearing on animals, insects, Indians.

American Oil Company
  555 Fifth Avenue
  New York, N.Y. 10017
        Large space map.

American Optometric Association
  7000 Chippewa Street
  St. Louis, Mo. 63119
        Posters pertaining to vision and reading.

American Petroleum Institute
  1271 Avenue of the Americas
  New York, N.Y. 10020
        Charts and maps, in color.

American Podiatry Association
  Mr. George Dame
    20 Chevy Chase Circle, N.W.
    Washington, D.C. 20015
        Posters on foot care.

American Seating Company
  901 Broadway Avenue, N.W.
  Grand Rapids, Mich. 49504
        A series of posture posters.

American Society for the Prevention
  of Cruelty to Animals
    441 E. 92nd Street
    New York, N.Y. 10028
        Posters advocating kindness to animals.

Armour and Co., Public Relations Dept.
  8849 S. Greenwood
  Chicago, Ill. 60619
        Map of the United States showing food sources.

Artext Prints, Inc.
  Westport, Conn. 06880
        Portrait prints, reproductions of works by old masters.

Association of American Railroads,
  School and College Service
  Public Relations Director
    Transportation Building
    1920 L Street, N.W.
    Washington, D.C. 20036
        Posters and booklets on railroads and railroading.

Automobile Manufacturers Association
  320 New Center Building
  Detroit, Mich. 48202
        Maps featuring the significant role played by trucks in distributing American products, and natural resources used in producing motor vehicles.

Bausch and Lomb, Inc.
  635 St. Paul Street
  Rochester, N.Y. 14605
        Wall chart relating to the microscope.

Better Vision Institute, Inc.
  230 Park Avenue
  New York, N.Y. 10017
        Charts and booklets related to eye care.

Bicycle Institute of America, Inc.
  122 E. 42nd Street
  New York, N.Y. 10017
        Posters on bicycle safety.

Book Enterprises, Inc.
  310 E. 44th Street
  New York, N.Y. 10017
        Portfolio of portraits of the Presidents. (Includes presidential fact-finding wheel, recording of Declaration of Independence by President John F. Kennedy, and large chart depicting development of the American flag). Also, portfolio of 18 Audubon bird prints, in color, and Currier and Ives "Four Seasons of the Year" prints.

Borden Chemical Division (Borden, Inc.),
  Consumer Services
    350 Madison Avenue
    New York, N.Y. 10017
        Chart showing journey of milk through pasteurization and processing; also, chart indicating temperatures at which various bacteria which may be found in milk are killed.

Bristol-Myers Products Division,
  Educational Service Department
    470 Mamaroneck Avenue
    White Plains, N.Y. 10605
        Charts: "Dental Health" and "Personal Grooming," primarily designed as teaching aids.

Buck Hill Associates, Dept. A
  Garnet Lake Road
  Johnsonburg, N.Y. 14084
        Posters and handbills of the 18th and 19th centuries, relating to America's past social and political history.

Careers, Inc.
1211 10th Street, S.W.
Largo, Fla. 33540
Career-oriented posters.

Cereal Institute, Inc.
135 S. La Salle
Chicago, Ill. 60603
Color chart with illustrations of wheat, barley, corn, oats, etc.

Chesapeake Bay Foundation, Inc.
17 State Circle, Box 1709
Annapolis, Maryland 21404
Posters, booklets and leaflets pertaining to conservation of the Chesapeake Bay area.

Civic Education Service, Inc.
1735 K Street, N.W.
Washington, D.C. 20006
"The U.S. in Facts and Figures," "U.S. Presidents" and "A World of Facts." Also, charts relating to countries of Central and South America.

C.G. Conn, Ltd.
1101 E. Beardsley Avenue
Elkhart, Ind. 46514
Charts relating to musical instruments, and some musical facsimiles.

Denoyer-Geppert Co.
5235-59 N. Ravenswood Avenue
Chicago, Ill. 60640
Illustrated booklets, maps, globes and charts.

De Witt Merchandising,
the Broadcasting Division, Inc.
227 E. 45th Street
New York, N.Y. 10017
Great Headlines — important newspaper pages through the years.

Farm and Industrial Equipment Institute
410 N. Michigan Avenue
Chicago, Ill. 60611
Illustrated wall chart pertaining to the evolution of farm and agricultural machinery.

Federal Reserve Bank of New York
33 Liberty Street
New York, N.Y. 10005
Money booklets.

Florida Citrus Commission, Box 148
1115 E. Memorial Boulevard
Lakeland, Fla. 33801
Colorful citrus posters.

Ford Motor Co., Educational Affairs Dept.
The American Road
Dearborn, Mich. 48121
Chart tracing this country's growth from 1838 forward; wall chart illustrating Ford automobiles from 1896; chart illustrating steps in assembling the modern car; chart showing the origins of units of measuring, and modern measuring devices; posters relating to the moon and space exploration.

Freedom House, Inc.
20 W. 40th Street
New York, N.Y. 10018
Famous Words of Freedom — quotations by great men.

Friendship Press
475 Riverside Drive
New York, N.Y. 10027
Map of Latin America, showing political divisions, geographical features, flags, etc.

Garden Club of America,
Conservation Committee
598 Madison Avenue
New York, N.Y. 10022
"The World Around You" — an educational packet.

General Electric Co.,
Space Technology Center
King of Prussia, Pa. 19406
Maps and charts relating to space flight and lunar exploration.

General Mills, Inc.,
Department of Public Service
9200 Wayzata Boulevard
Minneapolis, Minn. 55426
Pamphlets and folders on nutrition.

General Motors Corp., Public Relations Dept.
General Motors Building
Detroit, Mich. 48202
Charts dealing with the automotive industry; "Automobile Story Kit".

Goodyear Tire and Rubber Co.
1144 E. Market Street
Akron, Ohio 44305
Poster, "Automobiles".

Hagstrom Map Co., Inc.
450 W. 33rd Street
New York, N.Y. 10001
Decorative and historical maps.

Hamilton Watch Co., Public Relations Dept.
4 Corporate Park
Harrison, N.Y. 10528
Chart, "The Ages of Time," in color.

Harvey House, Publishers
S. Bukhout
Irvington, N.Y. 10533
Geological time chart.

Heckman Bindery, Inc.
908 N. Sycamore Street
North Manchester, Ind. 46962
Poster featuring the Caldecott Medal.

Hershey Foods Corp., Educational Dept.
19 E. Chocolate Avenue
Hershey, Pa. 17033
Colorful wall chart illustrating the production of Hershey cocoa and chocolate.

Institute of Life Insurance
277 Park Avenue
New York, N.Y. 10017
Posters related to family and finance.

International Bank for
Reconstruction and Development
1818 H Street, N.W.
Washington, D.C. 20006
Posters dealing with the work of the World Bank.

International Silk Association
299 Madison Avenue
New York, N.Y. 10017
Chart showing designers' sketches of women's fashions.

Kenworthy Educational Service
138 Allen Street
Buffalo, N.Y. 14201
Posters, cutouts, relating to animals, health, circus, farm, etc.

Laymen's National Bible Committee, Inc.
71 W. 23rd Street
New York, N.Y. 10010
Promotional aids for Sunday School Week and Bible Week.

Library Products, Inc.
Box 552
Sturgis, Mich. 49091
Posters and displays tying in with library services.

Manufacturing Chemists Association, Inc.
1825 Connecticut Avenue, N.W.
Washington, D.C. 20009
Charts; "Big Question of Science" and "What Science Means to You."

Manufacturers Hanover Trust Company
350 Park Avenue
New York, N.Y. 10022
World time chart.

Maryland Academy of Sciences
119 S. Howard Street (while new building is under construction)
Baltimore, Maryland 21201
Graphic Time Table of the Heavens.

Maryland State Drug Abuse Administration
2305 N. Charles Street
Baltimore, Maryland 21218
Directory of resources for drug abusers and their families.

Merck & Co., Inc.
126 E. Lincoln Avenue
Rahway, N.J. 07065
Chart of the elements.

Metropolitan Life Insurance Co.,
School Health Bureau
1 Madison Avenue
New York, N.Y. 10010
Health posters.

Metropolitan Museum of Art,
Department of Publications
Fifth Avenue and 82nd Street
New York, N.Y. 10028
Posters, prints, picture sets.

Michigan Historical Commission
208 N. Capitol Avenue
Lansing, Mich. 48933
Reproductions of paintings of important events in Michigan history.

National Academy of Sciences
2101 Constitution Avenue, N.W.
Washington, D.C. 20037
Posters.

National Aerospace Education Council,
616 Shoreham Building
806 15th Street, N.W.
Washington, D.C. 20005
"The Wright Brothers" — a portfolio relating to the Wright brothers and their accomplishments in aviation.

National Audubon Society, Charts Dept.
1130 Fifth Avenue
New York, N.Y. 10028
Charts featuring leaves, seeds, and other subjects of natural history.

National Coal Association
1130 17th Street, N.W.
Washington, D.C. 20036
Maps, charts and leaflets relating to coal.

National Commission on Safety Education,
National Education Association
1201 16th Street, N.W.
Washington, D.C. 20036
Safety posters.

National Cotton Council of America
1918 N. Parkway
Memphis, Tenn. 38112
Poster featuring the importance of fabric cleanliness.

National Geographic Society
17th and M Streets, N.W.
Washington, D.C. 20036
Reprints of magazine illustrations.

National Health Council,
Health Careers Program
1740 Braodway
New York, N.Y. 10019
Vocational posters dealing with health.

National Safety Council
425 N. Michigan Avenue
Chicago, Ill. 60611
Safety posters and pamphlets.

National Society for the Prevention
of Blindness, Inc.
16 E. 40th Street
New York, N.Y. 10016
Posters relating to eye care.

National Wildlife Federation
1412 16th Street, N.W.
Washington, D.C. 20036
Conservation directory; also, posters, booklets and leaflets pointing up the need for conservation of ecology and environment.

Natural Rubber Bureau
1108 16th Street, N.W.
Washington, D.C. 20036
Chart, "How Natural Rubber Is Grown".

New York Department of Commerce
99 Washington Avenue
Albany, N.Y. 12210
Posters.

New York Graphic Society
95 E. Putnam Avenue
Greenwich, Conn. 06830
Pictures representing book and nursery rhyme characters.

A.J. Nystrom and Co., Inc.
333 N. Elston Avenue
Chicago, Ill. 60618
Charts related to citizenship, science and other subjects.

Pan-American Coffee Bureau
1350 Sixth Avenue
New York, N.Y. 10009
Picture maps relating to the growth, production and distribution of coffee.

Panama Canal Information Office
Box M
Balboa Heights, Canal Zone
Folder with map, charts and photographs relating to the Canal.

Penn Prints, Inc.
221 Park Avenue, S.
New York, N.Y. 10003
Cavalcade of Early American Automobiles.

Perry Pictures, Inc., Dept. N-3
Malden, Mass. 02148
Reproductions of old masters.

Dr. Murray Politz
121 Congressional Lane
Rockville, Md. 20852
Posters on foot care.

Publishers Central Bureau
419 Park Avenue, S.
New York, N.Y. 10022
> Prints featuring Mother Goose, circus, and other subjects.

Regional Planning Council
701 St. Paul Street
Baltimore, Maryland 21202
> Directory of Environmental Resources in the Baltimore Region, compiled and published by the Baltimore Environmental Center, 112 E. 25th Street, Baltimore, Maryland 21218, and Health Council/Regional Planning Council, 701 St. Paul Street, Baltimore, Maryland 21202.

Revere Copper and Brass Co.
605 3rd Avenue
New York, N.Y. 10016
> Paul Revere pictures, in color.

Schmitt, Hall and McCreary Co.
110 N. 5th Street
Minneapolis, Minn. 55403
> Portrait prints of great composers.

School & Pre-School Supply Center, Inc.
Mr. Jack Faw, General Manager
5501 Edmondson Avenue
Baltimore, Maryland 21229
> Cutouts, pin-up and press-on letters in a wide range of sizes, alphabet and number cards, mini-posters, puzzles, jumbo patterns, flannel board sets, bulletin board kits, map studies, a diversity of large pictures and many other display items.

Science Associates, Inc.
230 Nassau Street
Princeton, N.J. 08540
> Cloud chart.

Scott-Foresman and Co.
1955 Montreal Road (Tucker)
Atlanta, Ga. 30311
> Posters, charts, literary maps of the United States; color chart on interplanetary travel, ocean depths, earth's surface, and others.

Scripta Mathematica
186th Street and Amsterdam Avenue
New York, N.Y. 10033
> Portraits of famous mathematicians.

Sonotone Corp.
P.O. Box 200
Elmsford, N.Y. 10523
> Charts related to the human ear and hearing.

Standard Brands, Inc., Educational Services
625 Madison Avenue
New York, N.Y. 10022
> Posters and charts related to bread materials.

Henry Stewart, Inc.
249 Bowen Road
East Aurora, N.Y. 14052
> Cut-outs of people in various countries.

Sunkist Growers, Inc.
P.O. Box 7888, Valley Annex
Van Nuys, Calif. 91409
> Posters relating to citrus fruits.

The Twentieth Century Fund
41 E. 70th Street
New York, N.Y. 10021
> Chart, "The Flow of Income and Expenditures in the United States."

United Educators, Inc.
801 Green Bay
Lake Bluff, Iowa 60044
> Posters.

United Nations, Sales Section
United Nations Plaza
New York, N.Y. 10017
> Multicolored chart showing flags of member nations.

United Nations Bookshop
United Nations Plaza
New York, N.Y. 10017
> UN posters, charts, miniature flags of member nations.

United States Steel Corp.,
Public Relations Dept.
71 Broadway
New York, N.Y. 10006

> Pictures, "Making Iron and Steel"; also, wall chart, "How Steel Is Made."

U.S. Department of Agriculture
A.R.S. Information
  Independence Avenue between 12th and
  14th Street, S.W.
  Washington, D.C. 20250
    Posters and pamphlets on nutirition.

U.S. Department of Agriculture
Forest Service
  Washington, D.C. 20250
    Maps, charts, posters, relating to trees,
    and forest regions of the United States.

U.S. Department of Commerce,
National Weather Service
  24th and M Street, N.W.
  Washington, D.C. 20235
    Daily Weather Map.

U.S. Department of Health,
Education and Welfare
  330 Independence Avenue, S.W.
  Washington, D.C. 20201
    Poster and leaflets relating to health.

U.S. Department of Labor, Women's Bureau
  Constitution Avenue and 14th Street, N.W.
  Washington, D.C. 20212
    Assorted folders and pamphlets.

U.S. Government Printing Office,
Superintendent of Documents
  Washington, D.C. 20401
    Charts illustrating safety with tools; fac-
    similes of U.S. Bill of Rights, Constitution
    and Declaration of Independence; hurri-
    cane tracking chart.

U.S. National Archives and Records Service
General Services Administration
  Pennsylvania Avenue at 8th Street, N.W.
  Washington, D.C. 20408
    Facsimiles of historic documents, photo-
    graphs, charts, including wall charts of
    the Constitution of the United States and
    the Declaration of Independence.

U.S. National Gallery of Art,
Publications and Information Services
  Washington, D.C. 20065
    Color reproductions.

U.S. Navy, Bureau of Naval Personnel
School and College Relations
  Washington, D.C. 20370
    Chart illustrating proper ways to display
    the American flag.

U.S. Treasury Department,
Savings Bond Division
  Washington, D.C. 20226
    Posters, leaflets, pamphlets related to
    savings bonds and stamps.

The Upjohn Co.
  7000 Portage Road
  Kalamazoo, Mich. 49002
    Color prints, famous men of science.

Ward's Natural Science Establishment, Inc.
  3000 E. Ridge Road
  Rochester, N.Y. 14622
    Chart outlining classification of the ani-
    mal kingdom.

Wheat Flour Institute
  14 E. Jackson Boulevard
  Chicago, Ill. 60604
    Charts depicting an enlarged wheat ker-
    nel, and flour-making processes.

Wilson and Co.
  Prudential Plaza
  Chicago, Ill. 60601
    Charts showing cuts of beef, pork and
    lamb.

Wine Institute
  717 Market Street
  San Francisco, Calif. 94103
    Map, "Wine Land of America".

World Confederation of Organizations
of the Teaching Profession
  1227 16th Street, N.W.
  Washington, D.C. 20036
    Wall charts relating to the daily life of
    school children in various countries.

POSSIBLE SOURCES OF FREE AND INEXPENSIVE DISPLAY MATERIALS

Part II

The names of the following plainly indicate the subject matter likely to be covered in any visual aids they may be able or willing to furnish. If there is a local branch, contact that first.

Aeroflot Soviet Airlines
   45 E. 49th Street
   New York, N.Y. 10017
Aerolineas Argentinas
   9 Rockefeller Plaza
   New York, N.Y. 10020
Aeronaves de Mexico
   500 Fifth Avenue
   New York, N.Y. 10036
Air Afrique
   683 Fifth Avenue
   New York, N.Y. 10022
Air Canada
   565 Fifth Avenue
   New York, N.Y. 10017
Air France
   1350 Avenue of the Americas
   New York, N.Y. 10019
Air India
   345 Park Avenue
   New York, N.Y. 10022
Air Jamaica
   545 Fifth Avenue
   New York, N.Y. 10017
Air New England
   East Boston, Mass. 02128
Air New Zealand, Ltd.
   245 Park Avenue
   New York, N.Y. 10017
Air Rhodesia
   535 Fifth Avenue
   New York, N.Y. 10017
Alaska Airlines
   200 E. 42nd Street
   New York, N.Y. 10017
Alitalia Airlines
   666 Fifth Avenue
   New York, N.Y. 10019
Allegheny Airlines
   80 E. 42nd Street
   New York, N.Y. 10017

American Airlines
   405 Lexington Avenue
   New York, N.Y. 10017
The American Bankers Association
   1120 Connecticut Avenue, N.W.
   Washington, D.C. 20036
American Federation of Labor and
   Congress of Industrial Organizations
   815 16th Street, N.W.
   Washington, D.C. 20006
American Forest Institute
   1835 K Street, N.W.
   Washington, D.C. 20006
American Forest Products Corporation
   2740 Hyde Street
   San Francisco, Calif. 94109
American Indian Historical Society
   1451 Masonic Avenue
   San Francisco, Calif. 94117
American Institute of Banking
   1120 Connecticut Avenue, N.W.
   Washington, D.C. 20036
American Institute of Cooperation
   1129 20th Street, N.W.
   Washington, D.C. 20036
American Iron and Steel Institute
   150 E. 42nd Street
   New York, N.Y. 10017
American Jewish Committee
   Institute of Human Relations
   165 E. 56th Street
   New York, N.Y. 10022
American Medical Association
   535 N. Dearborn Street
   Chicago, Ill. 60610
American Stock Exchange
   86 Trinity Place
   New York, N.Y. 10006
Anti-Defamation League of B'Nai B'Rith
   315 Lexington Avenue
   New York, N.Y. 10016
Association of American Railroads
   Public Relations Department
   1920 L Street, N.W.
   Washington, D.C. 20036
Australian Consulate General
   636 Fifth Avenue
   New York, N.Y. 10020
Austrian Airlines
   545 Fifth Avenue
   New York, N.Y. 10017

Austrian Information Service
    31 E. 69th Street
    New York, N.Y. 10021
Belgian Consulate General
    50 Rockefeller Plaza
    New York, N.Y. 10020
Brazilian Government Trade Bureau
    551 Fifth Avenue
    New York, N.Y. 10017
British Information Service
    845 3rd Avenue
    New York, N.Y. 10022
British Overseas Airways Corporation
    245 Park Avenue
    New York, N.Y. 10017
British Tourist Authority
    680 Fifth Avenue
    New York, N.Y. 10019
Bulgarian Legation
    2100 16th Street, N.W.
    Washington, D.C. 20009
Canadian Government Travel Bureau
    1771 N Street, N.W.
    Washington, D.C. 20036
Canadian Pacific Air
    581 Fifth Avenue
    New York, N.Y. 10017
Caribbean Island Airlines
    200 Park Avenue
    New York, N.Y. 10017
Chamber of Commerce of the United
    States
    1615 H Street, N.W.
    Washington, D.C. 20006
China Airlines
    60 E. 42nd Street
    New York, N.Y. 10017
Chinese Information Service
    100 W. 32nd Street
    New York, N.Y. 10001
Committee for a National Trade Policy,
    Inc.
    1028 Connecticut Avenue, N.W.
    Washington, D.C. 20036
Committee for Economic Development
    477 Madison Avenue
    New York, N.Y. 10022
Continental Airlines
    9 Rockefeller Plaza
    New York, N.Y. 10020

Czechoslovak Airlines
    545 Fifth Avenue
    New York, N.Y. 10017
Danish Information Office
    280 Park Avenue
    New York, N.Y. 10017
Delta Air Lines
    551 Fifth Avenue
    New York, N.Y. 10017
Dow Chemical Company
    Midland, Mich. 48640
Dow Jones & Company, Inc.
    Educational Service Bureau
    22 Cortlandt Street
    New York, N.Y. 10007
E.I. du Pont de Nemours & Company
    Du Pont Building
    Wilmington, Del. 19898
East African Airways Corporation
    576 Fifth Avenue
    New York, N.Y. 10036
Eastern Airlines
    10 Rockefeller Plaza
    New York, N.Y. 10020
Ecuatoriana Airlines
    500 Fifth Avenue
    New York, N.Y. 10036
Edison Electric Institute
    90 Park Avenue
    New York, N.Y. 10016
El Al Israel Airlines
    850 Third Avenue
    New York, N.Y. 10022
Ethiopian Embassy
    2209 Wyoming Avenue, N.W.
    Washington, D.C. 20008
Finnair-Finnish Airlines
    10 E. 40th Street
    New York, N.Y. 10016
The Foundation for Economic Education,
    Inc.
    30 S. Broadway
    Irvington-on-Hudson, N.Y. 10533
French Cultural Services
    972 Fifth Avenue
    New York, N.Y. 10021
German Information Center
    410 Park Avenue
    New York, N.Y. 10022

Greek Embassy
     2211 Massachusetts Avenue, N.W.
     Washington, D.C. 20008
Greyhound Bus Lines (Western Canada)
     Travel Bureau, 222 1 Avenue, S.W.
     Calgary, Canada
Guatemalan Air Lines
     501 Fifth Avenue
     New York, N.Y. 10017
Honduras Airline
     501 Fifth Avenue
     New York, N.Y. 10017
Iberia Air Lines of Spain
     97-77 Queens Boulevard, Rego Park
     Flushing, N.Y. 11374
Icelandic Airlines - Loftleidir
     610 Fifth Avenue
     New York, N.Y. 10020
India Tourist Office
     19 E. 49th Street
     New York, N.Y. 10017
Indonesian Embassy
     2020 Massachusetts Avenue, N.W.
     Washington, D.C. 20036
Institute of Life Insurance
     277 Park Avenue
     New York, N.Y. 10017
Iran Air
     345 Park Avenue
     New York, N.Y. 10022
Irish International Airlines
     564 Fifth Avenue
     New York, N.Y. 10036
Italian Government Travel Office
     630 Fifth Avenue
     New York, N.Y. 10020
Japan Air Lines
     655 Fifth Avenue
     New York, N.Y. 10022
Japan Information Service Center
     2 W. 59th Street
     New York, N.Y. 10019
Japan National Tourist Organization
     45 Rockefeller Plaza
     New York, N.Y. 10020
KLM Royal Dutch Airlines
     609 Fifth Avenue
     New York, N.Y. 10017
Korean Information Office
     1145 19th Street, N.W.
     Washington, D.C. 20036

Lacsa Airlines (of Costa Rica)
     500 Fifth Avenue
     New York, N.Y. 10036
Lufthansa German Airlines
     1640 Hempstead Turnpike &
     E. Meadow
     Hempstead, N.Y. 11554
Malaysia-Singapore Airlines
     500 Fifth Avenue
     New York, N.Y. 10036
Maryland Department of Economic
Development
     Tourist and Publicity Division
     Annapolis, Maryland 21401
Morocco Embassy
     1601 21st Street, N.W.
     Washington, D.C. 20009
National Aeronautics and Space
Administration
     400 Maryland Avenue
     Washington, D.C. 20546
National Airlines, Inc.
     219 E. 42nd Street
     New York, N.Y. 10017
National Association of Real Estate Boards
     155 E. Superior Street
     Chicago, Ill. 60611
National Council on Alcoholism
     2 Park Avenue
     New York, N.Y. 10016
National Dairy Council
     111 N. Canal Street
     Chicago, Ill. 60606
National Education Association
     1201 16th Street, N.W.
     Washington, D.C. 20036
The Negro Bibliographic and Research
Center, Inc.
     117 R Street, N.E.
     Washington, D.C. 20002
The Netherlands Information Service
     711 Third Avenue
     New York, N.Y. 10017
New York Stock Exchange
     11 Wall Street
     New York, N.Y. 10005
New Zealand Embassy - Information
Department
     19 Observatory Circle, N.W.
     Washington, D.C. 20008

Nigerian Embassy
    1333 16th Street, N.W.
    Washington, D.C. 20036
North Central Airlines
    666 Fifth Avenue
    New York, N.Y. 10019
Northeast Airlines
    299 Park Avenue
    New York, N.Y. 10017
Northwest Orient Airlines
    537 Fifth Avenue
    New York, N.Y. 10017
Norwegian Information Service
    825 Third Avenue
    New York, N.Y. 10022
Norwegian National Tourist Office
    505 Fifth Avenue
    New York, N.Y. 10017
Olympic Airways
    888 Seventh Avenue
    New York, N.Y. 10019
Ozark Air Lines, Inc.
    Public Relations
    1740 Broadway
    New York, N.Y. 10019
Pakistan International Airlines
    545 Fifth Avenue
    New York, N.Y. 10017
Pan American World Airways, Inc.
    Pan American Building
    New York, N.Y. 10017
Penn Central Transportation Co.
    Public Relations Department
    466 Lexington Avenue
    New York, N.Y. 10017
Pharmaceutical Manufacturers Association
    1155 Fifteenth Street, N.W.
    Washington, D.C. 20005
Philippine Air Lines
    30 Rockefeller Plaza
    New York, N.Y. 10020
Philippine Tourist and Travel Association
    170 24th Avenue
    San Francisco, Calif. 94121
Piedmont Airlines
    666 Fifth Avenue
    New York, N.Y. 10019
Polish Airlines Lot
    500 Fifth Avenue
    New York, N.Y. 10036

Portuguese Government Tourist
    Information Bureau
    570 Fifth Avenue
    New York, N.Y. 10036
President's Council on Physical Fitness
    and Sports
    400 6th Street, S.W.
    Washington, D.C. 20024
Puerto Rico Government Travel Bureau
    8 W. 51st Street
    New York, N.Y. 10020
Royal Jordanian Airlines
    280 Madison Avenue
    New York, N.Y. 10016
Sabena Belgian World Airlines
    720 Fifth Avenue
    New York, N.Y. 10019
Saudi Arabian Airlines
    880 Third Avenue
    New York, N.Y. 10022
Scandinavian Airlines
    138-02 Queens Boulevard
    Jamaica, New York 11435
Scandinavian National Tourist Offices
    505 Fifth Avenue
    New York, N.Y. 10017
Seaboard World Airlines, Inc.
    100 E. 42nd Street
    New York, N.Y. 10017
Small Business Administration
    1441 L Street, N.W.
    Washington, D.C. 20005
Social Security Administration
    (Obtain related publications from your
    nearest Social Security Administration
    office)
South Africa Information Service
    655 Madison Avenue
    New York, N.Y. 10021
Southern Airways, Inc.
    80 E. 42nd Street
    New York, N.Y. 10017
Southern Railway System
    Southern Railway Building
    920 15th Street, N.W.
    Washington, D.C. 20005
Spanish Embassy, Cultural Relations Office
    1629 Columbia Road, N.W.
    Washington, D.C. 20009

Swedish Information Service Travel
  Information
    825 Third Avenue
    New York, N.Y. 10022
Swiss National Tourist Office
    608 Fifth Avenue
    New York, N.Y. 10020
Swissair
    608 Fifth Avenue
    New York, N.Y. 10020
Synthetic Organic Chemical Manufacturers
  Association
    1075 Central Park Avenue
    Scarsdale, N.Y. 10583
Tax Foundation, Inc.
    50 Rockefeller Plaza
    New York, N.Y. 10020
Thailand - Royal Thai Embassy
  Office of Public Relations
    2300 Kabrama Road, N.W.
    Washington, D.C. 20008
Trans-Australia Airlines
    230 Park Avenue
    New York, N.Y. 10017
Trans International Airlines
    350 Fifth Avenue
    New York, N.Y. 10001
Trans World Airlines - Promotion
  Department
    605 Third Avenue
    New York, N.Y. 10016
Turkish Tourist Information
    70 Fifth Avenue
    New York, N.Y. 10011
Union Pacific Railroad
  Advertising Department
    345 Park Avenue
    New York, N.Y. 10022
United Air Lines
  Sales Promotion Department
    P.O. Box 66,100
    Chicago, Ill. 60666
United Arab Airlines
    720 Fifth Avenue
    New York, N.Y. 10019
United States (Steamship) Lines
    1 Broadway
    New York, N.Y. 10004
United States Savings and Loan League
    111 E. Wacker
    Chicago, Ill. 60601

United States Steel Corporation
  Educational Services, Public Relations
  Dept.
    71 Broadway
    New York, N.Y. 10006
Venezualan Government Tourist Bureau
    485 Madison Avenue
    New York, N.Y. 10022
Western Air Lines
    609 Fifth Avenue
    New York, N.Y. 10017
World Airways, Inc.
    666 Fifth Avenue
    New York, N.Y. 10019
Yugoslav Airlines - JAT
    509 Madison Avenue
    New York, N.Y. 10022
Yugoslav Information Center
    488 Madison Avenue
    New York, N.Y. 10022

BOOK WEEK AIDS

Children's Book Council, Inc.
  175 Fifth Avenue
  New York, N.Y. 10010
        Posters, streamers, signs, etc., to promote
        Book Week and children's reading generally

SPECIAL EXHIBITS

ALA BOOKLIST (for list of varied
  exhibition sources)
    50 E. Huron Street
    Chicago, Ill. 60611
The American Institute of Graphic Arts
    1059 Third Avenue
    New York, N.Y. 10021
National Library Week (Sponsored by the
  National Book Committee in cooperation
  with the American Library Association,
  usually in April)
    1 Park Avenue
    New York, N.Y. 10016
Travel Exhibition Service
  Smithsonian Institution
    Washington, D.C. 20560

Mentioned here are items used by or known to the Enoch Pratt Free Library's Public Relations Division. Readers familiar with others may wish to expand the list. Those who have no access to local graphic arts shops or stationery stores, may write for samples, catalogs, prices or other information, if they feel so disposed.

Acetate Sheets

(Clear, transparent composition, .005 thick. Can be cut into strips ½" wide, the ends secured together with OK clips and the loop thus formed used to hold open books or pamphlets without obscuring illustrations or printed matter. Available in 20" x 50" sheets, or 40" x 50' rolls.
Almac Plastics of Maryland, Inc.
6311 Erdman Avenue
Baltimore, Maryland 21205
(Or by the yard, 40" wide)
Becker Sign Supply Company
321 N. Paca Street
Baltimore, Maryland 21201

Adhering Solution

Graphic arts supplier

Art Gum

Graphic arts supplier or stationery store

Beaverboard

(Pressed paper wall board about ¼" thick. Used as base for cutting decorations, as well as for caption letters. Smooth surface. May be purchased in sheets 4' x 8' and up)
Lumber companies

Book-saver (Liquid plastic)

Delkote, Inc.
76 S. Virginia Avenue
Penns Grove, N.J. 08069

Cardboard

(22" x 28", 6-ply, for small posters)
Mudge Paper Company
1400 Russell Street
Baltimore, Md. 21230
(28" x 44", 14-ply, for large posters, decoration and showcards)
Becker Sign Supply Company
321 N. Paca Street
Baltimore, Md. 21201

Cardboard Cutter (Jacques Shear)

Hobbs Manufacturing Company
666 Lincoln Street
Worcester, Mass. 01605

Cases (Glass, portable)

Michaels Art Bronze Company
Kenton Lands Road
Erlanger, Ky. 41018

Remington, Rand
1290 Avenue of the Americas
New York, N.Y. 10019

John E. Sjörström
1717 N. 10th Street
Philadelphia, Pa. 19122

Cloth

(Suede finish for covering tables and other display surfaces, 54" wide)
Becker Sign Supply Company
321 N. Paca Street
Baltimore, Maryland 21201

Cutawl Machine

The Cutawl Corporation
Bethel, Conn. 06801

Display Fixtures

(Book racks, other racks, peg board, panels, tables, etc.)
Demco Educational Corporation
2120 Fordem Avenue
Madison, Wis. 53704

Dur-O-Peg
3039 W. Carroll Avenue
Chicago, Ill. 60612

Masonite Corporation
29 N. Wacker Drive TR-10
Chicago, Ill. 60606

Mitchell Folda-Leg Tables
Walcott-Taylor Company, Inc.
4925 St. Elmo Avenue, Beth.
Washington, D.C. 20014

RTC Industries, Inc.
920 W. Cullerton Street
Chicago, Ill. 60608

Display Units

Design & Production, Inc.
6001 Farrington Avenue
Alexandria, Va. 22303

Wiremasters
3702 S. Iron Street
Chicago, Ill. 60609

Film (Silk screen)

Graphic arts supplier

Film-Stencil Knife

Hardware Store

Gem Clips

Stationery store or graphic arts
supplier

Glue

(Furniture, for silk screen frame)
Hardware store

Hinges (Metal)

Hardware store

Inks (Lettering)

Graphic arts supplier

Insulite

(Wood pulp wall board, in burlap or
smooth finish. May be purchased in
sheets 4′ x 8′ or larger)
Lumber yard or mill

Lacquer Thinner

Graphic arts supplier

Lettering Guide

Wrico Lettering Stencil
Wood-Regan Instrument Company,
Inc.
184 Franklin Avenue
Nutley, N.J. 07110

Letters

(Cut-out. Write for catalogs and price
lists)
ABC Letter Company
5301 N. Kedzie
Chicago, Ill. 60625

Artype, Inc.
345 E. Terra Cotta Avenue
Crystal Lake, Ill. 60014

Florida Plastics Midwest, Inc.
10224 S. Kedzie, Evergreen Park
Chicago, Ill. 60642

Gaylord Bros., Inc.
7272 Morgan Road
Liverpool, N.Y. 13088

House of Letters
10224 S. Kedzie, Evergreen Park
Chicago, Ill. 60642

Krasel Industries
514 Blackwelder
Los Angeles, Calif. 90016

McLogan Supply Company, Inc.
1324 S. Hope
Los Angeles, Calif. 90015

Mitten's Display Letters
85 Fifth Avenue
New York, N.Y. 10003

(Pin-up and press-on letters)
School & Pre-School Supply Center, Inc.
5501 Edmondson Avenue
Baltimore, Maryland 21229

(Stencils of letters and numbers)
Stencil-Art Publishing Company
44 Harrison
Cleveland, Ohio 44146

Tablet and Ticket Company
1021 W. Adams Street
Chicago, Ill. 60607

Tablet and Ticket Company
1250 Wilshire Boulevard
Los Angeles, Calif. 90017

West-on-Letters
132 S. La Brea Avenue
Los Angeles, Calif. 90036

OK Clips

Stationery store

Paints (Cold water)

(Iddings, and similar coatings. Manufactured in paste form and mixed with water by user — approximately one pint water to quart of paste. Variety of colors)
Graphic arts supplier, or hardware store

Paints (Poster)

Graphic arts supplier

Paints (Silk screen)

Graphic arts supplier

Paper

(Brown, gummed, for the backs of cardboard decorations, to join the pieces together)
Industrial Paper Company
4718 Hollins Ferry Road
Baltimore, Maryland 21227

Paper

(Brown, wrapping, for patterns. Roll, 36″ width, 50 lb. weight)
Matthew C. Fenton, Inc.
1525 W. 41st Street
Baltimore, Maryland 21211

Industrial Paper Company
4718 Hollins Ferry Road
Baltimore, Maryland 21227

Pins

Graphic arts supplier or stationery store

Plywood

Lumber company

Projector (Enlarging)

Charles Beseler Co.
219 S. 18th Street
East Orange, N.J. 07017

Opa-Scope
Projection Optics Company, Inc.
271 Eleventh Avenue
East Orange, N.J. 07018

Rubber Cement

Graphic arts supplier

Sign Machines

Line-O-Scribe
Morgan Sign Machine Company
4510 N. Ravenswood Avenue
Chicago, Ill. 60640

Printasign
Reynolds Printasign Company
9830 San Fernando Road
Pacoima, Calif. 91331

Showcard Machine
Showcard Machine Company
318 W. Ohio Street
Chicago, Ill. 60610

Silk Screen Printing Frame

Graphic arts supplier

Silk Screen Stencil Silk

(12xx, meshes 124 per inch)
Graphic arts supplier

Solvent (Silk screen paint)

Graphic arts supplier

Squeegees

Graphic arts supplier

Stapling Gun, Staples

Graphic arts supplier or stationery
store

Tacks (Thumb - white, black and colors)

Five-and-dime or variety store,
graphic arts supplier or stationery
store

Tacks (Upholstery)

Hardware store

Tape (Adhesive, clear)

Stationery store or graphic arts supplier

Tape (Cloth, adhesive)

Fastape
Demco Educational Corporation
2120 Fordem Avenue
Madison, Wis. 53704

Tape

(Cotton, various widths, white and colors,
in spools of 1,000 yards each. Useful for
tying books open, and attaching books to
display backdrops)
Wick Narrow Fabric Company
124 E. 7th Avenue
Conshohocken, Pa. 19428

Tape (Masking)

Graphic arts supplier

The following have appeared within the last decade or so, prior to this revision's publication. The list is by no means complete, but includes items to which we have had access. In a few instances works are presented for their good ideas, despite inadequate artistic execution.

BOOKS

Ballinger, R.A.
Lettering Art in Modern Use
Student edition '65 Van Nos - Reinhold

Biegeleisen, J.I.
The ABC of Lettering
4th edition '71 Harper

Bowers, M.K.
Easy Bulletin Boards for the School Library
'66 Scarecrow

Brantlinger, Fred
Easy-to-Make Bulletin Boards
'63 Hayes School Publishing Co.

Brinkley, John, ed.
Lettering Today
'65 Reinhold

Carmel, J.H.
Exhibition Techniques
'62 Reinhold

Carr, Frances
Planned and Illustrated Bulletin Boards
'64 Hayes School Publishing Co.

Coplan, Kate
Poster Ideas and Bulletin Board Techniques: For Libraries and Schools
'62 Oceana

Coplan, Kate and Rosenthal, Constance
Guide to Better Bulletin Boards
'70 Oceana

Currie, Dorothy
Making Dioramas and Displays
'62 and '65 The Instructor Curriculum Materials Handbook Series

Garvey, Mona
Library Displays: Their Purpose, Construction and Use
'69 Wilson

Hayett, William
Display and Exhibit Handbook
'67 Reinhold

Koskey, T.A.
Bulletin Board — Idea Sources
'62 Fearon

Lee, C. and L.
The Fourth Grade Bulletin Board Guide
'64 Denison

Mathre, T.H.
Bulletin Boards in Color
'69 Denison

Rice, Charles
Reading and Library Bulletin Boards
'66 Hayes School Publishing Company

Thompson, C.L.
Language Arts Bulletin Boards
'65 and '67 Fearon

Tschichold, Jan
Treasury of Alphabets and Lettering
'66 Reinhold

BOOKLETS, ARTICLES

A. Bartnofsky
Unusual Art Exhibit; a Community Mental Health Center and a Library Work Together
Westchester Square Branch of the New York Public Library
Il Wil Lib Bul 46:532-5 F '72

Book Displays in Banks Promote Interest in Reading
Il Pub W 182:42-4 D 24 '62

J.W. Bryant
Greenwich Reading Time
Il Wil Lib Bul 40:530-1 F '66

Bulletin Board Displays
Il Wil Lib Bul 42:86-7 S '67

N.H. Carrier
Three Christmas Windows; Easy, Effective and Cheap
Il Pub W 202:40-2 Ag 21 '72

Dallas Public Library
Displays: The Book As Art
Il Wil Lib Bul 42:334-5 N '67

E. Friese
Charlotte's Web; Example for Librarians,
Lib J 87:273-4 Ja 15 '62

M. Garvey
Bulletin Board Display; Using Large
Circles As Background Design
Il Wil Lib Bul 43:776-7 Ap '69

M. Glaser and J. Snyder
Letters and Imagination
Il Am Artist 34:14 N '70

M. Gray and R. Armstrong
Lettering for the Public Image
Design 64:120-3 Ja '63

G.F. Horn
Bulletin Boards; How to Make Yours
Come to Life
Il Design 64:28-30+ S '62

Ideas for Summer Displays
Il Wil Lib Bul 40:966-7 Je '66

J.S. Lorr
Lettering, Art Curriculum Stepchild
Il Design 70:10-14 Sum '69

G. Martin
Turkey on the Bulletin Board
Il Lib J 87:3626-9 O 15 '62

Red Ink on Green Paper; Lists and
Exhibits before the Public in December,
(compared with the rest of the year)
Il Lib J 94:4117 N 15 '69

A.R. Schiller
Art of Library Science Exhibit; Using
Library of Congress Classification System
Il Am Lib 3:184-5 F '72

P. Vandervoort
Calligraphy in the Curriculum, 2d ed
Il Sch Arts 70:34-6 D '70

INDEX

CALENDAR NOTES

CALENDAR NOTES

CALENDAR NOTES

CALENDAR NOTES

CALENDAR NOTES

CALENDAR NOTES